BECOMING AN IRONMAN

BECOMING AN IRONMAN®

FIRST ENCOUNTERS WITH
THE ULTIMATE ENDURANCE EVENT

Edited by Kara Douglass Thom

BREAKAWAY BOOKS
HALCOTTSVILLE, NEW YORK
2002

Becoming an Ironman: First Encounters with the Ultimate Endurance Event

Hardcover ISBN: 1-891369-24-5

Paperback ISBN: 1-891369-31-8

Library of Congress Control Number: 2001088409

"Ironman" is a registered trademark of the World Triathlon Corporation.

Published by Breakaway Books
P.O. Box 24
Halcottsville, NY 12438
(800) 548-4348
www.breakawaybooks.com

ACKNOWLEDGMENTS

Special thanks to Victor Douglass, from whom I inherited the urge to write; my parents for their abundant generosity; my Tía Dorothy Osborne for telling me she intended to read a book of *mine* one day (this is as close to a book of poetry as I may get); my husband, Mark—his verve for the sport has rubbed off and made me a better competitor; in fact, helped me become an ironman athlete; my personal editors who provided valuable input after the "first read"—Carolyn Douglass, Jackie Campbell, Bill Shirer, and Janice Kennedy Singer (and thanks Jan for introducing me to triathlon); Kari Riley for helping me meet my deadline; Rob Docherty, Xtri.com founder and ironman resource extraordinaire; Christina Gandolfo, editor of *Triathlete* magazine, for answering my steady stream of questions; my friends at the Dallas County Medical Society for their support; my training partners who made sure I stayed in reasonable shape by meeting at *my house* at 6 A.M. to run; and the ironman athletes from around the world who shared their versions of 140.6 miles. There were many more stories than could be published, but every single one was a winner, just like the athletes themselves.

—K. D. T.

CONTENTS

GOLDEN FINISH

I CAN

THE EARLY YEARS

AROUND THE WORLD

JOHN COLLINS
Founder of the Ironman Triathlon

Ironman triathlon has always affected its participants more deeply and in more varied ways than almost any other individual-participation sport. Each competitor brings to the starting line his or her particular background, character, and training readiness. The finish line (or the medical tent) sees a different person, forever altered by the crucible that is the ironman.

I was fortunate to be in on the beginnings not only of the Ironman, but also modern triathlon itself. My wife, Judy, and our two children, Kristin and Michael, were competitors in the San Diego Track Club's pioneering event at Mission Bay, San Diego, California, in September 1974. A few months later we dragooned the Optimist's Club of Coronado, California, into initiating what is now the longest-running triathlon in the world. In 1977 the idea for the Ironman was born during an awards party in Hawaii. The first running was in 1978, which was also my first ironman. I finished ninth out of twelve finishers and learned a lot about myself, some parts of which I might have wished to remain hidden.

The first ironman experience remains vivid in memory even for those who have completed dozens of events. That initial look at what is actually down inside can be frightening, uplifting, or even comical. Ask any ironman veteran about that first attempt and he or she will be able to recount the entire event in infinite detail. The wife of an old friend from the early days of ironman had a rule: Her husband was not allowed to talk about an event for a longer period than it took to complete the event. Luckily for some of us at the back of the pack, an ironman gives us plenty of time to talk!

Kara Thom has assembled a collection of recollections from a broad spectrum of iron veterans. You will recognize many of the names, but some of the most moving come from names you will not have seen before, but may well not forget. Each has stepped into the furnace and come out the other side a changed person. Not all finished the first try, but all gave it the best they had in them on that day. No matter how many times they complete the event, each can only complete the first one once.

Strap on the heart-rate monitor, lace up the running shoes, get yourself a bottle of electrolyte drink and a couple of energy bars, and sit back to enter the special world of the iron virgin!

KARA DOUGLASS THOM

The sport of triathlon, as we know it today, is less than twenty-five years old, so most triathletes older than thirty came to the sport via some other athletic avenue. I kicked off my athletic lifestyle with ballet. I transitioned into aerobics but feeling the urge to be outdoors, began fitness walking, which shifted to running, and, finally, the metamorphosis to triathlon. My husband's triathlon roots start with basketball. I have friends who are gymnasts turned triathletes, cyclists turned triathletes, divers turned triathletes; and there is even the rare hybrid, couch potato turned triathlete. Triathlon comprises a veritable melting pot of athletes. And that is how it should be, because ironman-distance triathlons started as a contest among athletes of different backgrounds.

In 1978 John Collins, a U.S. Navy Officer, challenged swimmers, cyclists and runners to test their fitness against each other. He organized an event that combined all three of Honolulu's endurance races: the Waikiki Rough Water Swim, a 2.4-mile open-water swim, the Around Oahu Bike Race, a 112-mile cycling race that originally spanned two days, and the Honolulu Marathon, 26.2 miles of running. Fifteen men competed in the original Ironman race on February 18, and at the end of the day twelve called themselves ironmen. Today there are more than thirty-five ironman-distance triathlons around the world, but the most prestigious remains the Hawaii Ironman.

As varied as our athletic histories are, so too are our personal backgrounds. And while the least common denominator of all ironman-distance triathlons is 2.4 miles of swimming, 112 miles of biking and 26.2 miles of running, every race experience is unique. What athletes bring to the starting line in terms of who they were before they began training for this beast—family history, work pressures, aspirations, and fears—combine to make each ironman race as dynamic and distinct as their DNA. Sure, there are places in this book where ironman finishers will say "aha!" from the knowing, the empathy of a common feeling or shared experience in training or racing. But it's the people behind every finisher's medal that make the story compelling beyond the enormity of covering the distance on human power. And each has a lesson that isn't necessarily applicable only to the person competing. These nuggets are what make the ironman experience entertaining for anyone—from those who've been there and done that to those who never will, but especially for those who aspire to it.

I had the privilege of hearing nearly two hundred first-time ironman tales, and it was difficult to whittle this book down to the stories published herein. Stories came by way of e-mail, telephone, and face-to-face interviews in brewpubs, hotel lobbies, kitchen tables, and living rooms. I strived to keep each story as close as possible to the way it was told to me, to preserve the voice of the storyteller. For that reason you many note word usage and spelling variations not prevalent in American English. People represented in this book live across the globe, and I used *their* words. If readers of this book don't feel like they're experiencing the race firsthand, I figure I want them to feel like they're *hearing* it first-hand, as I did. Thanks to all who contacted me and provided such rich material.

Trying to corral these stories into sensible categories was another challenge. Many stories fit into more than one—for instance, Bill Bell belongs in both "Early Years" and "Golden Finish." My intent was to group tales of a similar aspect of the race—age, finish time, place in geography, or place in history—that can connect readers to what they have or may experience. Anyway, it was my attempt to put these stories in a logical grouping and I think every ironman finisher will fit in one if not more of these categories.

Another challenge was the word *ironman* itself. Ironman is now a trademark of the World Triathlon Corporation, and when used in reference to races held by the WTC it should be capitalized. But many triathletes use *ironman* in a general sense as a noun (a usage that predates the race by a century or two), or as an adjective, as in "ironman-distance triathlon," because there are such races that aren't official "Ironmans." So throughout the book, I do not capitalize the word *ironman* when used in this sense; I capitalize it only when it is part of the title of a WTC race or when referring to the Hawaii Ironman.

There are plenty of triathlon books out there that can help you become a triathlete, help you train better and race faster. But very few tell you what it *feels* like—really give you the dish on what goes on inside a triathlete's head. If that's why you're reading this book, then additional required reading includes Mike Plant's *Ironwill*, and *Triathlon: A Personal History*, by Scott Tinley. Both of these books will give you a sense of where this sport has come from and why it compels people to do it. Of course, another great ironman read is the fabled 1979 *Sports Illustrated* article by Barry McDermott (May 14, 1979). This is worth searching through the microfiche for at your local library. All were great references for me when I needed background, or needed to fill in a missing link on someone's faded memory.

Plus, unlike many of the triathlon books out there, they address the sport on an emotional level.

And emotion is really what you get when you cross the finish line. I believe ironman-distance races have grown to the extent they have not because of some athletic boom, not because people suddenly want an exorbitant challenge, but because the experience purges emotion in a way that improves our human condition and clarifies our existence. It changes us. I am hard pressed to explain that further. So are all the other people represented in this book. It changes us beyond making us fitter, leaner, and aerobically superior. Of all the ironman athletes I talked to while compiling this book, not one of them said they would never do another. Not one. The compulsion, I believe, isn't in the exercise; it's in the emotion.

The essence of the emotion of each story of each lesson of each person is what I've tried to wrap words around to create this anthology of first-time ironman experiences. Journey through time, across the globe, and to extraordinarily high endorphin levels. See if you can feel it.

FUN-CORE FINISHERS

Not too fast, not too slow. Just right.

HAPPY BIRTHDAY TO ME

ED RANKIN

DATE OF BIRTH: MAY 20, 1970

RACE: IRONMAN CALIFORNIA 2000

TIME: 11:25:54

On May 20, 2000, I turned thirty while I slept. At 4:30 A.M. my wake-up call rang. I'm pretty sure I was already awake. I had slept surprisingly well considering the day that awaited me, but pre-sunrise quiet mixed heavily with my nervousness and I gathered what I needed as if still dreaming.

I left my brother and sister sleeping while I walked to Denny's for breakfast. I chose Moon Over My Hammy from the menu instead of a more orthodox pre-race meal like oatmeal, bagels, or yogurt. I wouldn't eat solid food again for a long time. A few hours later I'd eaten, driven with my brother and sister to the swim start, and struggled into my wet suit and bright red latex cap. My parents, whose flight from Washington, D.C., had been delayed, would arrive sometime during the bike leg.

My family didn't know this was a big deal at first, and neither did I. I didn't ask them to come. All I knew was that I would be racing for about twelve hours and they would see me for maybe ten seconds. And I knew it was an expensive proposition—my parents and sister coming from D.C., my brother from San Francisco—I never even mentioned it. It was my sister who rallied the troops. My older sister, the organizer of people, herded them along. I'm sure they had no choice. But as it turned out, they enjoyed it, and for me, having my family there was a huge part of my ironman experience.

I joined the mass of fifteen hundred identically clad athletes and shuffled toward the ramp into the water. Just before I reached the water, I turned to see my brother standing at the ramp with tears in his eyes. I don't know if he was proud of me or afraid for me, but the emotion was infectious and I began to worry I'd fill up my goggles from the inside.

It was only three years ago, while at lunch with my dad, that I first considered taking on the distance. I was telling him about my cousin Michael, who had done ironman several times and had done it well. I was trying to explain to him what an accomplishment that was. He just shook his head and said, "Do me a favor. Tell me you won't ever do that." That probably cemented it for me. I'm not a rebellious kid and I don't have anything to prove to my dad, but I knew I couldn't make that promise.

Now my dad was on his way to watch his youngest son compete in an ironman triathlon. He probably thought he might as well watch his son bang his head against a wall. It's a difficult thing to do, but why would you do it?

All Good People like to eat.
Every person who is hungry is a good person.
Every person who is not hungry is a bad person.
It is better to be hungry than rich.

This mangled syllogism hangs, framed, on the dining room wall of one of my favorite places in the world. I've been reading it and absorbing it into my consciousness since I was five years old. I'm not sure when I realized it was meant to be funny and not necessarily words to live by, or if I've even realized it yet. I like to eat and I still think it's a good thing.

Lots of people like to eat, or claim to, but my family has a fondness for mealtime that I think goes unrivaled in the civilized world. I hear people talking about the kitchen being the social center of their house and that the togetherness found at mealtime, the warmth, the relaxed conversation are so enjoyable, so important. That's nice, and I agree to a point, but for me it comes down to chewing and swallowing. The act of shoveling it in really does something for me. I love to eat an elegant gourmet meal with friends or family but I also enjoy eating an entire package of Tuna Helper with double the butter by myself. I figure I'm just an especially good person.

Being that much of a good person didn't seem to come with consequences until I was about eleven. I weighed sixty-five pounds for years. I remember sitting next to my father, who was well over three times my size, and matching him fork for fork at dinner. The hollow leg jokes were old by the time I was seven. Then, around sixth grade, I developed a nice little spare tire, my face began to get puffy, and soon I filled out into a full-blown fat kid. Being a fat kid in junior high school kind of sucks, and I knew being a fat kid in general would suck. I also knew I couldn't wait for it to get better.

I went to Weight Watchers for the first time in eighth grade. I think my undiscriminating pleasure in solid food helped me to succeed at first. Having never been exposed to them before, I didn't recognize low-fat vegetable spreads, turkey lunch meats, and fat-free mayo as the poisonous crap they probably are. I was trying to come to grips with the notion that good people like to eat small portions and they like to stop eating well before it hurts. I began to try to believe I was a bad person for getting so much enjoyment out of stuffing myself. Thus began about fifteen years of alternately living a life I enjoyed, and dieting.

In college I found a really cute girlfriend who didn't seem to mind my bulk or my enthusiasm at the trough. She was what some people would call an enabler. She used to speak endearingly about my bellies. I was living happily in denial, however, until the day I went to The Gap to get a new pair of jeans. Unable to help me, they suggested I try a specialty store to find my size. I had gotten used to being directed to the "husky" department as a youngster, but being directed to a completely different line of retailers was a little more than I could take. I stopped drinking beer for a while, reduced my portions, ate less frequently, and once a week I fasted for an entire day. I was miserable, but the pounds fell off. Somehow I was able to drop to a less-than-obese weight and stay there for a number of years. But I still thought of myself as a fat kid, and mealtime was always an occasion for painful choices.

It wasn't until I was twenty-six that a coworker casually laid the answer on me. "Hey Ed, wanna run in the Cherry Blossom ten-miler this spring?" he asked. Somebody else inside took over, and I heard myself say, "Yeah, sure, sign me up." Somehow I knew immediately what I had gotten myself into, and the thought of a grueling and humiliating unprepared race day had me making and sticking to a regular running schedule.

I was still a big guy, however, and the lower half of my body began to make its displeasure at my new lifestyle known. First I got shinsplints, then kneesplints, then thighsplints, and then I got hipsplints, too. I would eat three or four Advil before a run, at least as many after, and several in between so I could walk normally. Finally even they weren't doing the trick anymore. It was time to stop running for a while. I had been a competitive swimmer as a kid, and it was once one of those things I was almost good at. So it was an easy substitution for me to make. I swam three or four times a week and then eased back into running. Soon I was running NSAID-free and feeling pretty good. Race day came and couldn't have been better. I was a qualified member of a group of six thousand fitness enthusiasts, athletes. That day I was pretty sure I wasn't a fat kid anymore.

Soon after, I realized that without entry in another race—paid for and marked on my calendar—I couldn't make myself exercise regularly. Triathlons had always seemed to speak to me, even as a youngster. I think I must have seen coverage of one of the first Hawaii Ironman competitions. A dream of doing something like that had been with me from an early age, but so was the dream of being president or an astronaut or the most popular kid in school. It was just a fantasy I could indulge in if I had a few minutes to myself. But here I was in pretty good running shape and decent swimming shape. I figured, 'Anyone can ride a bike; it might even be a nice resting leg between a hard swim and run.' Again my coworker suggested a race, and a couple of months later I was ready for my first triathlon. My swimming ability and nonchalant approach to the bike led to the slightly frustrating experience of watching most of the field whiz by me as I searched in vain for an easier gear. But I made up some ground on the run, and by the end I knew I wanted to do this again, I wanted to do it better, I wanted to do it harder. I wanted to be a tri-geek.

I swam more than two and a half miles on a mismeasured course in a very cold Pacific Ocean. I was relieved. The mass 'combat swim' wasn't nearly as rough as I had anticipated—a couple of kicks and punches, but still a peaceful swim for the most part. Some efficient volunteers stripped me of my wet suit and helped me find my swim-to-bike bag. I changed, found my bike amid the hundreds of others and began a journey into the unknown: a 112-mile ironman bike leg. I had biked more than one hundred miles before, but never with the intention of saving just enough energy to run a marathon when I was finished. I felt pretty good but I knew the day had just begun. With the swim done it was tempting to think of my first ironman as one-third complete, but I knew I had more than ten hours to go with less than two down.

On the backside of the bike course we rode through the 'M.A.S.H.' mountains—you see them during the opening cuts of '*M.A.S.H.*'—sort of scrubby. I heard my number called for the special-needs bags, but I never got it. That was okay. I didn't really know what to put in a special needs bag anyway. I missed out on some Advil, Gummy Bears, and a few GUs. My only real problem on the bike was overhydration. As instructed by my coach and my cousin, I didn't get off the bike to pee and it made me feel like, 'Yeah, this is pretty hardcore.'

In 1999, after a few years of two or three short-course triathlons each summer, I moved to Boulder, Colorado. I didn't move there for the purpose of training, but I quickly met a lot of people who did. I did the Boulder Peak, an Olympic-distance triathlon, and decided I wanted to get a little more serious. I was only toying with the idea of doing an ironman when I brought up the Ironman California web page in early September. Two details struck me like a hammer. First, race day was my thirtieth birthday, and second, registration was closed. According to the web page, the race was full. These facts pulled me off the fence. I was going to do an ironman, and I was going to do Ironman California. I e-mailed the organizers and learned that a few slots were left, but I would have to send my registration overnight.

The day my race application was accepted, I got a coach. All I had to do was what she told me to do. She would know if I was working too hard and be able to scale me back, and I didn't have to worry I wasn't doing enough. I could also feel comfortable that the work I was doing was preparing me specifically for an ironman. She had me lifting weights, doing track workouts and interval training, which I previously had known nothing about. We had nine months to work together until race day, and that would be just enough.

Around 2:30 P.M. I finished the bike in just under six hours. I was pleasantly surprised to learn that, relative to the rest of the field, my biking had been stronger than my swimming. It was hilly, and I think training in Colorado had given me something of an advantage. Other than spending too much time relieving myself and getting stung by a bee, it was almost embarrassing how trouble-free my day was going. Happy birthday to me . . .

The biggest unexpected problem had come three weeks earlier when I quit my job as a network administrator after my boss refused to give me time off for the race. I had been talking about ironman since September, when I signed up. As it was, we weren't seeing eye to eye, so I gave him my two weeks' notice. My employer decided it was a security risk to have me around and paid me to go home. I took the opportunity to drive to San Diego, stopping at as many national parks as I could squeeze in before arriving at the starting line.

In transition a saintly iron volunteer sat next to me in the changing tent, laying out my running gear. He opened up my package of two Advil and brought me a cup of water as I changed. Another two volunteers wiped me down with sunscreen and I was off. Within a mile or two I came around a corner to see my whole family waiting for me. They were all a bit annoyed that I wore what everyone else seemed to be wearing: black shorts, white tank, and white hat. Regardless, they found me and erupted into cheers. My sister pulled in next to me to provide a little running company. When she let me go a couple of miles later, I knew I'd pass them three more times before the day was through. This shrank the run down into short segments of anticipation. I refueled on their enthusiasm and support with each pass. I'm sure I was hurting, but I couldn't feel it.

When I'd begun training my coach asked me what my goals were. One thing I told her was that I wanted to finish with a good time. Especially, I didn't want to walk. She rolled her eyes. Still, I felt conflicted about walking. But I knew, like she knew, I'd hurt myself worse without the breaks, without walking the hills.

On my third pass by the family, my brother joined me. He had never run more than a mile and a half in his life, and I was grateful for what I figured would be several hundred yards of company. Six or seven miles later he said he couldn't run anymore and he'd see me at the finish. I don't know if having my brother and sister run with me constituted the illegal acceptance of outside emotional aid, but we didn't get caught and it made all the difference in the world.

In the last couple of hundred yards to the finish I felt like I was on brand-new legs. I sprinted through the chute with my arms above my head like I'd just won the thing. The organizers even held up tape for me to break. Less than eleven and a half hours. I didn't really know what that meant, but I knew I was happy. My body didn't quite know how to react to the emotion.

I was awarded a finisher's medal and T-shirt on the spot and directed to the massage tent. After a short but much-needed massage, I rejoined my family and remembered, 'Oh yeah, it's my birthday.' Suddenly I was in the mood for some solid food and a beer. They treated me to dinner at the Chart House, which was on the run course. As we left, there were people still running the race and the accomplishment began to sink in. I was proud of myself and I let myself feel proud. I did and always will have done this race. Even if I go up to 230 pounds again, I'm still an ironman.

After Ironman, Ed took the scenic route back to Boulder via Disneyland and more national parks. He adopted Molly, a lab-mix puppy, and eventually found another job. Ed has remained at 'fighting weight' and continues to train for triathlons. He plans to take on Ironman Canada next.

ALL IN THE FAMILY

TIM BURGESS AND SUSIE BURGESS

DATES OF BIRTH: JUNE 15, 1963

   AND JULY 21, 1961

RACE: IRONMAN USA 1999

TIMES: 11:54:09 AND 14:16:53

W e have five kids. Brook, our oldest, was eight at the time, and our youngest, Wyatt, was one. We signed up for the inaugural Ironman USA in Lake Placid while we were en route to do our first triathlon. Yes, that's right. We dropped our applications in the mail, *then* attempted our first sprint triathlon.

I'm a chef and own a restaurant; Susie stayed home full time with the kids. At the time, my business was well delegated and Susie was looking to get out of mommy shape and into real fitness condition. I told her I'd hire help with the kids so she could train—she'd never had full-time help with the kids before. It might be appropriate to add here that Susie was a closet smoker.

Thanks for sharing, Tim. It's pretty unusual for people to have five kids these days, and when we signed up, even though people were saying, "That's a pretty big thing, and you haven't even done a race yet," I think we both, in our hearts, knew we were determined and would be able to do it—no matter the obstacles. We've been through a lot of obstacles businesswise and kidwise and we're both able to handle a lot of stress and are good at dealing with that.

A good friend of ours had done Ironman Canada a couple of times and she said, "I'll do a plan for each of you." It looked manageable. I'm sure when anyone looks ahead at their game plan it seems manageable. But it was pretty insane. We had three kids in school, so we had to juggle getting them ready in the morning and picking them up and Tim getting to work. Originally we thought, 'Oh, Tim and I will train a lot together.' It would be a good husband-and-wife accomplishment, having this goal together. It ended up that we tag-teamed training. We had planned this nice, long bike ride every week that we'd do together, and I think that happened once. I would get up around 4 A.M. and ride my bike to swim. I'd usually get my stuff done by the time the kids were going to school. Tim did his training in the evening. We did a tremendous amount of juggling.

Especially so because my business got crazy. I became short staffed and had to work the open shifts myself, sometimes putting in sixty hours a week at work. We ended up canning the au pair four weeks after hiring her when we discovered she was sleeping on the job. Turns out it was like having one more child—and we were better off without an eighteen-year-old to complicate matters.

We thought it couldn't get any worse. The light at the end of the tunnel was the race. Susie and I planned to leave the kids at home. A trip and a goal just for the two of us. Then there was the night Susie's mom called.

At the time my mom had been diagnosed with ovarian can-cer—she has since passed away—so her offering to watch the kids was a pretty generous thing. She was calling to tell me she didn't feel as though she and my dad would be capable of watching five little kids. That was okay. I could completely understand. I could deal with that. But five minutes later Tim called to tell me one of his chefs just left—he was throwing up blood and he sent him to the hospital.

At that point, we thought, 'This is a joke.' After all the tremendous amount of training, it was coming down to the wire. The next two weeks we were under so much emotional pressure and to top it off, we didn't even know if we would be able to do the race. Are we in? Are we out? Is Tim in? Am I out?

For a while we thought only one of us could do it. I felt like Susie trained so hard and she got up early every morning for the last year. She deserved to do the race. I know I would have felt tremendous guilt if I were the one doing it. This was happening four weeks before the race. We were completely burned out.

But then I had a really long ride to do and I just blew it off. The next day I rode, but during my ride I convinced myself I wouldn't go. When I got back, Tim had written me this note, it was very motivational. "We've come this far, let's stick together. We can pull this off. If Lake Placid was tomorrow, we could do it." We persevered through the training. Now it was getting there. I think we both knew that once we got there, we could do the race. We'd done the training, but now we were faced with the actual journey of physically getting from Charlottesville, Virginia, to Lake Placid.

With five kids . . . and no baby-sitter.

Right. So I called around in Lake Placid, thinking it wouldn't be a problem. "I'll be able to find a baby-sitter just for the race. It'll be fine." I came up empty handed. Plan B was to bring our own. We had this wonderful babysitter for a couple of years who would come every other Sunday, and she's a close friend of our family. Robin was going back to college, and we had to entice her to postpone it for a week. We told her she would have much more fun going on an adventure with us. I'm sure it was the craziest trip she's ever been on.

For starters, she didn't know what an ironman was. But even before learning firsthand, she had to drive fourteen hours with all of us to get there. We were like the Griswolds going to Walley World. Three adults, five children, enough gear for two ironman triathletes packed in a Suburban. Every time we stopped we had to unpack everything to get in and out. We were squished. I'm sure it looked hysterical. God, it was a long drive.

We were trying our best to entertain the kids as we went along. The last part of the drive, we went to Hershey Park in Pennsylvania and had a day of roller-coaster rides. Fortunately the kids are used to a lot of confusion. We finally made it to Lake Placid and pulled in to the motel to check in. Originally, we had a reservation for two. The woman looked at me and said, "That many people can't stay in your room." We thought, 'Here we go again.' We ended up getting a second room and once we unpacked, life got a little normal.

Well, normal is having our kids all over us anyway. It was probably good not to have any kind of expectation except to finish and to feel good finishing it. With all the stuff thrown at us, we were both thrilled to be there.

Race morning Tim and I said a prayer down by the water and then we struck out on our own to find good places to start. I got stuck in a group of people who were pretty aggressive with a lot of physical contact. Tim, I don't believe, had that. I thought I was in the right place, but I got in a bad spot. The first lap was very physical; the second lap was much better. I got into a rhythm and that's probably pretty typical on a two-lap course.

I came out of the water about ten minutes after Susie. That's how we've done it pretty much every race. For us, that's really fun. I'm always looking for her. It took me longer than I thought to catch her.

He always underestimates my biking ability.

I broke the bike down into ten-mile segments. Finally, at mile forty—on the first loop—I saw her. "You doing okay?" I said as I pulled up beside her.

I thought, 'Oh no, he's got me!' Right when he passed me, there was this big climb and I thought I could try to stick with him. That lasted for about three seconds and I decided to return to my zone again. It's so interesting the difference between Tim and me. He's looking at his odometer; I'm looking at the view. He and I are very different—just our whole training philosophy. I do this stuff because I love it. I enjoy it. It's a good, healthy diversion for me. It's a good mental thing. It's a good physical thing. I have a tendency to focus on my surroundings rather than focus on the race.

I lollygagged in the transition, but not as much as Susie. She had someone give her a neck massage and a foot massage. Her transition was almost twenty minutes.

My neck was killing me after that ride! I was so excited being inside the tent. I was so caught up in the moment. New socks and suntan lotion and hat and sunglasses and make sure that you don't leave anything behind! Here we are, these fruitcake people who had never done a triathlon before, signing up for ironman. I have to say out of all distances, I really do love the longer races—it's just so much more interesting. There's such camaraderie. In the whole race, there's this whole sense of people pulling together to get each other through it. I think that's the interesting difference between people who are the professionals or people trying to qualify, and the people who are doing it for a life experience—that there's this incredible sense of everybody wanting everybody to complete it.

I agree. You may not be able to draft, but you can draft on that good energy. There is definitely a sea of energy rushing toward the finish line. All you need to do is hop on for the ride.

The sad thing is, some people don't. When I went out on the run, I felt good at the beginning. I had just gotten my neck massage and I felt great. But there was this grouchy guy I hooked up with and he just wasn't good to be around. I literally went as fast as I could to get away from him. Then I didn't see him again. I guarantee that guy didn't finish the race.

The only weird thing I had happen on the run—and I wish I had been prepared for it—was I got a bad blister at mile fourteen. I've had blisters before and not thought much of them because I knew I could stop and deal with it. But I didn't have any Band-Aids and neither did any of the aid stations.

All of a sudden I realized I was going to have to walk. I looked at my watch and thought, 'Well, I can finish by walking.' But I was a little frustrated. As people passed me, I'd say,

"Excuse me, does anybody have a Band-Aid?" There was this woman—her name was Robin—she said, "You know what? I've got some moleskin."

"Oh, you're a savior!"

I spent ten minutes in an ambulance getting my foot fixed. From that point I was able to run. I hobbled a little bit, but I was happy for the rest of the race.

The course was like a figure eight so Susie and I saw each other quite a bit on the run. There was a bridge right before mile ten where I saw a man—his number was 669—and he said, "Your wife said to jump on you and hold you down till she catches up."

Then I'd see the man and I'd say to him, "You didn't get him this time. You better get him, Hon. You better keep him down." So Tim and I saw each other on the run, how many times?

Three times.

Yeah, three times, and we'd give each other high fives and kisses and it was so exciting to be there—doing this ironman, when we weren't even sure we'd get to the starting line.

While Susie was dealing with her blister, I was dealing with cramps. I was trying to guess how much sodium to take. I think I was overhydrated and really started slowing down.

Oh, poor baby. You were so slow.

My whole theory was, 'This is ironman!' It wasn't a marathon, not a PR 10K. Bad things will happen and you simply have to deal with it and keep moving.

Yeah, don't worry about it. That's part of the deal. There's going to be some pain.

Running that last lap through the stadium was euphoric. Every frustration, every thought of quitting, all the training problems, all the baby-sitter problems, the problems with work, they all went away during that last lap.

That's right, by then we both thought, 'Who cares?'

As I got closer to the finish line I could feel the energy from the cheering like an electric current. Every person who crosses the finish line raises the energy meter of the crowd one more notch. I had a guy right in front of me so I stopped and let him go through, then I went on and crossed the line—I wanted it all to myself!

Tim got to finish when it was light out. When I had about six miles to go they started cranking up the generators to light the course. All of a sudden I realized, 'God, it would have been really nice if I had packed a long-sleeved shirt in my special-needs bag.'

The last part of the run into town is uphill. By the time I got to the speed-skating oval, I was so psyched. I was definitely putting along, but I felt good and I was running. There was a wild crew and music playing. There was so much energy in that place. It was so loud. The later you finish, the better the party.

That was a party. It was past 9 P.M. and the kids were troupers. We were waiting for Susie about one hundred meters from the finish. When I saw her I encouraged the four older kids out on the track to run in with her.

We had one who wasn't going to come. Devan didn't want to come with me. "Come on with Mommy," I said, "Mommy is going to carry you." I had four of the kids—three of them running and me carrying Devan—she's my daughter, who, at that time, was three. Fortunately I was feeling good. The other three kids—my oldest son and then there's a daughter and then a son, we go boy, girl, boy, girl, boy—honest to God think they're in a race. It was hysterical. I had Eliza holding my hand, pulling me, and the boys, Travis and Brook, were a little bit ahead. I could sense they understood what it was all about. During the day they'd see us coming and going, but at that point it all came together. They had seen Tim finish. So here they were, they ran across the finish line with me and I swear, to them that was the greatest thing—for me and for them.

I told Tim it was the closest he was ever going to come to having a baby. Ironman is similar to having your first baby—being in labor that long and dealing with all the pain.

We felt so amazing afterward.

You know what it is? It's being able to set a goal and have the goal be really hard and planning it far in advance and having to deal with all the crap that comes up. That, in itself, makes an ironman so much sweeter.

After we got through that we realized we could pretty much do anything we wanted to do. It's a definite 'I can' issue.

It has been the greatest thing in the world for our kids, espe-

cially for our daughters, to see that their mom can do stuff like
that. It's neat for them to see, and it's also neat for other moms
who may be supporting their husbands through racing. Those
moms might think, 'Hey, I can do it, too.' Just because you're a
mom doesn't mean you can't be an ironman.

*Although Tim and Susie enjoyed their joint ironman finish, next
time they've decided to sign up for different races.*

BROTHERLY LOVE

MICHAEL ARENBERG

DATE OF BIRTH: JUNE 17, 1959

RACE: IRONMAN CANADA 1990

TIME: 11:35:54

When I got into triathlon it was ironman from the beginning. I came home from college and my dad and I watched ABC's *Wide World of Sports*. He was working a crossword puzzle, and I was reading a book and watching out of the corner of my eye. It was something called Ironman and a woman named Julie Moss was crawling to the finish. By that time we were both transfixed—we put down what we were doing and watched with amazement. I turned to my dad and said, "I'm going to do that someday." He gave me one of those looks, like, 'Yeah, sure.'

That finish became tattooed on my brain. I wanted to know more. A friend of mine started doing triathlons, and he helped me get started. I was intimidated and scared, but I entered Ironman Canada right off the bat and signed up to do two other Olympic-distance triathlons before that.

My friend gave me advice. "You can't just step into an ironman in your first year."

I said, "Why not?"

"You need to take your time and build up to it with smaller triathlons."

"Why?"

He couldn't come up with an answer, but he told me I was crazy. Now, with my physiology background, *I'm* the one telling people, "Wait a minute; you've just started triathlon. There's no way you're ready to enter an ironman."

I trained hard, but it was all guesswork. I bought a bike and taught myself to swim. The week before I was to do my first triathlon, which was six weeks before the ironman, I tore my hamstring playing softball (the same day I had run twenty-four-miles). Obviously, I didn't do that triathlon. The next race was two weeks later. I did the swim but was afraid to bike or run for fear of making my injury worse.

Nobody in my family knew what an ironman was, aside from my dad, and all he knew was that Julie Moss had crawled across the finish line. There was no going around with pride saying, "My son is doing an ironman," because he didn't quite understand my desire to do that.

Then somebody from work told my older brother Tom, "Do you know what your brother is doing?" That day my brother called and said, "You need someone there with you. There's no way you're going to do this alone."

I spent five days in Penticton by myself before Tom arrived. I was locked in my condo freaking out. 'My God, what am I doing here?' The reality of the event started to hit me, and the excitement and the energy and the nerves began to build, and it was the longest five days I can remember. I saw all these other fit people and realized, 'I'm very normal here.' When I was home training for the ironman, I was part of an elite group. I was very unnerved by how average I felt.

Tom and his wife, Diane, and their kids showed up the day before the race. My brother was there; I felt better, I felt secure.

We said good-bye near the giant peach—which is a landmark

for triathletes, but normally serves as a refreshment hut of sorts for beachgoers. I was surprised at all the emotion. Saying goodbye to him brought tears to my eyes. The reality of the event, the fear of what that day was going to bring was slapping me in the face. I had a huge amount of anxiety about attempting a marathon on a leg that I'd only recently been able to run a limping, sore five miles on.

The swim was a frightening experience for somebody who had never swum in a mass start. I was swimming for my life and getting hit a lot. In the scramble my watch got knocked off. I wonder if it's still running at the bottom of Okanagan Lake. A short while later I hit somebody or something. I don't know to this day what I hit, but it broke my hand.

I was far enough to the left that I kicked my way toward a kayak. I had to regroup for a second. The person on the kayak said, "You okay?" I said I was and went to join the pack again. It was like looking for an entrance onto a highway when you're merging.

I swam the rest of the way but had a hard time keeping my fingers together. Pulling through the stroke was painful. I didn't know it was broken until a couple of days later when I had it X-rayed.

I got out of the swim and volunteers took the wet suit off. I had my hands braced on the grass as they dumped me on my butt and whipped off the wet suit. My bathing suit came off to my thighs. I squirmed on the ground trying to put my bathing suit back on and ran to the changing tent very disoriented.

I tried to remember all that I had rehearsed as far as changing. I dumped everything out on the ground and had no idea what to do. 'Get the bike shorts on, jersey on, shoes on in the tent.' I ran out and made contact with my brother just outside the transition.

To have somebody there, even though I didn't see him much during the race, to know he was waiting for me, was comforting. And to hear his voice, "Go Michael," was what I needed to stay motivated.

He thought his role was to document. He videotaped and took still pictures, holding one camera against his eye and aiming the other camera toward me. I'm sure there were other people around him, but in my mind he was standing there alone. I saw him, I gave him a thumbs-up, and away I went on the bike.

I had heard Richter Pass was tough. I knew because at registration I eavesdropped. I was shy about letting anybody know this was my first triathlon and didn't want to ask questions so I stood by the question-and-answer table for half an hour and just listened. I heard a guy say, "It's an overrated climb, it's in stair-step fashion; don't worry about it." And that took the weight of the world off my shoulders because I had heard it was a seven-mile climb. I didn't suffer on the bike until after Richter Pass; my knee especially started to hurt.

But waiting for me in my special-needs bag were Pop Tarts and Mountain Dew. There were no gels or six to twelve percent carbohydrate solutions that were as well designed as they are now. Gatorade was good, and I drank that, but there was no plan with what to eat, how much to eat, when to eat. I just ate and drank when I felt like it.

I assumed I was going to see Tom on the course more often than I did. Eighty miles into the bike I thought, 'Where the hell is my brother? I need him out here." I saw him, finally, at Yellow Lake. I went screaming by and he jumped in the car and drove up to another point. My left knee was throbbing. On the video you hear, "Go Michael," and me saying, "My left knee is," and it ends. Watching the video it's obvious what word was going to come out, but fortunately there wasn't any tape left.

The last twelve miles I felt like I hardly moved. I remember seeing the lead runners coming in as I finished the bike, and I recognized Ray Browning as the two-time champion. My impression was, 'Oh, my God. These guys look awful.' It was incredibly sobering because these were the pros going by. I thought, 'If they look that bad, this is going to be terrible for me.'

Starting the run I was in a foggy fatigue. I was not looking forward to the marathon. I was afraid of walking the whole marathon. I was afraid of how long it was going to take me to walk and whether I'd be able to walk, and I didn't want to walk. I wanted to run people down. Underneath my visor, I had a picture of my parents. I've made that a habit—it was my way of reminding myself to think of them being with me. I also had the names of my four brothers and sister, Bob, Tom, Doug, Jim and Mary; Grandma and Grandpa; and my nieces and nephews, Liz, Molly, Carl, and Emma. I had the whole family. I told them that if I wanted to quit or give up, I would imagine them cheering me on.

I needed the encouragement because I had never felt my legs that dead in my life. I went out through town and the only thing that kept me running, initially, was the fact that there were people there. I didn't want to walk in front of people.

The hamstring, actually, wasn't that bad the first couple of miles. I think I was more worried about why my quads were so shot. I'd never experienced this kind of fatigue before. The first couple of downhills were just terrorizing my quads. There was a double in-and-out. Halfway out to Skaha Lake we went into a neighborhood and did this long curlicue, all the way to a cone and I thought I'd never get there. Once I got to the cone, I realized I had to do that whole curlicue thing to get out of the neighborhood—it was one of the worst marathon courses I've ever been on. I made the decision to get a massage at that point because my hamstring was starting to throb. It was sending me painful little messages. I thought, 'Well, that's my hamstring tearing fiber by fiber.' Every time that would happen, I'd slow down to a walk, it would go away, and then I'd start running again.

At twenty-two miles there was a trailer, which was part of the aid station, and my hamstring was hurting so bad that I went behind the trailer, grabbed my leg like I was choking it, and squeezed the hamstring. I let out an angry scream. It was an 'I'm mad at feeling this bad' scream. I needed to release that tension, and then I continued on.

It was such an incredible fight over that last fourteen miles that I went across the finish line very blandly. I clapped my hands twice and raised my arms a little at the finish line and kept walking. There was no stalling out at the finish line. It just hadn't sunk in. Two people grabbed me, I got my medal, and reached down to take a look at it. It was just a simple, small M-dot.

When I finished I didn't want to go to the massage tent. I didn't want to go to the medical tent. I wanted to see my brother. I walked to the gate and he grabbed me and he was trembling, and he said, "I'm so proud of you."

What happened at that finish line that day welded us together forever, and I think he knew then and there that if I ever did one of these again, he was going to be there, and I knew I wanted him there.

I've done eight more—Canada again in 1991 and 1994, when I qualified for Hawaii. Went to Hawaii in 1994, 1999, and 2000; Germany in 1997; and Lake Placid in 1999 and 2000. Tom has gone to every one, including when he broke his foot. It was the day before we were supposed to leave for Canada and he broke his foot falling down the stairs. His doctor told him not to travel, but he went. And then going to Germany—he's got a wife, three children—but, "If Michael's going to Germany, I'm going with him."

I never went back and raced in a shorter distance triathlon. Just didn't see the need. All nine triathlons I've finished have been ironmans.

Michael Arenberg was a teacher in Wheaton, Illinois, when he completed his first ironman. He has since gone on to get a degree in exercise physiology and studied ironman triathletes and endurance exercise as part of his coursework. Now he puts that knowledge to use as a coach.

EARNING THE IRONMAN DEGREE

KEVIN JERMYN

DATE OF BIRTH: JUNE 29, 1957

RACE: GREAT FLORIDIAN 1997

TIME: 13:45:20

I'll never get used to those individual room air conditioner units that cut on and off every three minutes. Two nights before my first ironman I slept about two hours total, in fifteen-minute intervals. The night before I slept maybe three.

I wasn't scared. It wasn't impending doom that kept me awake. It was more childlike excitement. The impatience of eager anticipation for Christmas morning. This was something very new, very big, and something I had trained for all year and really looked forward to doing. Still the adult in me, the iron virgin, woke up worrying that I didn't get enough sleep.

"Are you worried about this?" I asked my friend Morrie, my training partner and roommate, who had traveled with me from Panama City to this event in Clermont, Florida. I told him I wasn't, which wasn't typical male bravado. I simply was approaching this event as yet another long training day. I was going to do the swim like I had always done the swim. I was going to do the bike like I had always done the bike, I was going to do the run however I could.

It was 4:30 A.M. I had two cups of coffee, grits, a muffin, and two Advil. We drove to the start at 5:30.

I always prepack my bags the night before. I have a big bag that everything goes in. And of course before I prepack it, I go through the transitions in my room. I put my wet suit on and act like I'm swimming. I take my bike stuff and put it on and go to the end of the driveway and back. I take off my bike clothes and change into my run stuff. Then I'll grab everything and put it in the bag. I check it three, four times. I open it, look inside, and zip it back up. Then I open it again because I'm so worried that I'll forget something. I think not having what I need is the only thing that could throw my day off.

When we got to the race site I delivered my special-needs bags—bike and run gear and food, which volunteers hand you at various places along the course—to their designated place in the transition area. I checked my bike one last time, got body-marked, and headed to the van for my wet suit.

"Morrie! My wet suit, I can't find my wet suit!" Panic set in as I ransacked the van. The race start was in forty-five minutes. I flailed and searched for another minute while wondering if it was worth the stress to drive back to the hotel—a fifteen-minute ride.

"Kevin." Morrie called my name from the front of the van. My wet suit hung on the van door, black as the early morning sky.

I downed a bottle of Gatorade and a Power Bar, put on my suit, and headed to the water's edge with fifteen minutes to spare.

We gathered on the shore of Lake Minneola and sang the national anthem in the dark. I stayed close to Morrie so I could say good luck one last time. You can never say that enough. I really wanted him to do well. As the clock ticked down, there seemed to be no sense of urgency to get in the water among the seven hundred participants. We all just stood on the beach.

"Go!"

We started walking slowly into the water, but everyone was still talking.

"You all ready to have a good day?" said someone behind me.

Yeah, I was ready for a good day.

I waded for about fifty feet and then got into the frenzy. I always seem to swim in what I call an iron cross—a person right, left, front and back of me. Everyone self-seeded real well. We were going the same pace. We were all in a groove. The buoys were easily visible on my left. The swim was a double loop of an elongated rectangle. At the corners were buoys that looked like volcanoes. They were especially beautiful as the sun began to rise and shine on them.

My swim cap was adjusted so that there was a rhythm from the water popping off my ear and I started listening to that. Like a metronome. I used that as a creative distraction.

My first loop took fifty-two minutes. The whole swim was surprisingly easy. I was mentally drifting off, relaxing really. On the second loop, I started preparing for the bike. That's probably what I dreaded the most. I had done the Assault on Sugarloaf (a bike rally that is the same bike course as Great Floridian) and it took a lot out of me. It was probably about ten degrees hotter when I did it. I was afraid I wasn't going to stick to my time.

When I came out of the water, a volunteer unzipped my wet suit and pulled the shoulders down. My time was 1:27:02. I ran across the grass and someone handed me my bag. In the changing tent someone helped me don my Century Gel biking shorts and white Coolmax sleeveless shirt. Other volunteers passed out food on trays. I drank my Boost drink from the bag and had some orange slices and a bite of crumb cake. Then I was off to get my bike.

I was at the back of the pack. I took it easy as I ate my breakfast—a PR Bar with two full bottles of Gatorade. My heart-rate monitor was on and working at 130 beats-per-minute. Most of my training was at 140 beats-per-minute and I didn't want it to go over 145. I had taken a fall on the bike two weeks prior, head over heels about fifteen miles per hour. I was drafting off Morrie and got too close to his rear wheel. I had the usual shoulder-and-side road rash with heavy bruising on the pelvis area and a serious pinpoint hit just above the right hip flexor. I had about half a cup of fluid drained from the impact spot a week before the race. It was tight and kept me from getting out of the saddle.

Steve passed me at mile ten. Morrie passed me at mile fifteen. I hit Sugarloaf Mountain at mile twenty. I couldn't decide if I should wear sunglasses. I kept going back and forth. Don passed me at mile thirty-five. Ten miles later I passed Don. He looked like he was going to have a long day.

Most of the ride is in the country—orange groves—but pretty boring terrain really. It's not one of the more scenic rides, but in every town we rode through, people lined the course and cheered.

I grabbed my special-needs bag at mile sixty-five, drank a strawberry Boost and ate four bites of coffee cake. Fifteen miles later I started to slow down. I contemplated eating a chocolate GU, something a cyclist friend had encouraged me to try for just this sort of moment. I decided to wait until mile one hundred, just in case it upset my stomach. It didn't, and sure enough it brought me back up. No surge of energy, just back to normal. I passed Steve and prepared for my next set of hills. After the last hill I was back at the lake. I had to put on double brakes all the way down for fear of flying across the highway. But once at the bottom I was on the run course and seeing people who were at least eight miles into the run, maybe farther because there were triple laps around the lake. With just four or five miles to the transition I knew I was going to finish the bike—it was a great feeling.

It was overcast and much cooler than when I rode the course a few weeks before. Still, I consumed a full water bottle and at least half of the race day sports drink between every aid station. This was probably one of the hardest things to do because I had to coast while relieving myself every ten miles or so. I ate about eight chocolate chip cookies, a Fig Newton, two peanut butter crackers, another PR Bar, two bananas, and a Power Bar spaced fairly evenly over the ride. Then there were the two Advil at mile ten and the two Aleve at mile ninety.

I started to think 'run' and to loosen up my legs. I waved to people running, sat up, stretched, and thought, 'Okay, what am I going to do on this jog?' I was so happy I made it that far: No flat, I didn't wreck, nothing went wrong, and my bike split was almost two minutes under my goal at 6:58:25.

A volunteer racked my bike in the transition; I grabbed my transition bag and went to the tent. I had never bricked in training. My longest run, fourteen miles, was about four weeks ago. I didn't plan on running the whole thing anyway.

On with Coolmax shorts, a water bottle fanny pack with two GUs (my new best friend), Advil, Aleve, and my trusty heart-rate monitor. I ate several orange slices and took time to visit the Port-a-Potti. I was planning on walking the first mile but I felt too good and decided to jog. My first mile was 9:25. Between mile one and two I saw Morrie heading back on the first five-mile out-and-back.

"Side cramps, I've gotta walk," Morrie said. "You'll probably catch me."

That didn't make sense at the time because he was running and I was walking.

There was a tremendous hill at mile two that almost everyone walked up. At this point I decided to walk up most of the hills and run down the hills and flats. I saw Steve about two miles behind me when I was at mile three and a half and saw Don about three miles behind me when I reached mile four. The seven-mile loop around the lake brought me to the transition area at mile twelve with a cumulative time of 10:48. Fourteen miles to go and three hours and fifteen minutes to make my goal of fourteen hours. I could probably do that walking, and the sun was still shining. It was 6:15 P.M.

Things started getting interesting as it got dark. Most of the run was in residential neighborhoods and as the sun went down I began to see people settling into their evening routines. Walking the dog, taking out the trash, leaving to go to the grocery store. By this time everyone is on their own. You're either in your groove or you're not. There was no sense of urgency because I wasn't trying to win, I just wanted to stay in control.

I walked until my heart rate dropped below one hundred and then I started to jog again. I walked through all the aid stations. By now I had eaten my two GUs. As it got dark, it got cool and the St. Pete Mad Dog aid station began to serve hot chicken soup. As I gulped it down I envisioned angels coming down from heaven, lifting me up, and carrying me to the next mile. My body was like a sponge; it soaked up the soup immediately and it went throughout my body. I had never had it before in training, especially when I was at that level of depletion. I flew on that for probably a mile or two.

I kept finding the same people along the course. We'd talk, and again I had no sense of urgency to finish. I'd rather talk to these people than pick up the pace. I was caught in the moment of being comfortable and happy. I was happy I wasn't hurt and happy I didn't care I wasn't going as fast I could. It made the whole experience easier. I was never thinking of the finish during the swim, during the bike; I was never thinking of the finish most of the time. I was just living in the moment. I had to be comfortable and in control the whole event. If I wasn't I had to slow down. And the more I thought that, the more I started to enjoy the experience.

I had such a respect for the distance, such an apprehension that I wouldn't make it through the whole thing, that I knew I had to take my time and have fun with it. My one goal was to finish and that was it, no matter how long it took.

That was the same attitude I had when I competed in my first triathlon. I had watched a triathlon in Panama City, where I live, and I was curious: Could I make it? I didn't care what time. I signed up for the Gulf Coast Triathlon, a half ironman, in 1990. I finished an hour or so ahead of the cutoff time. My curiosity returned every year, and I continued to sign up for that race.

My third loop was completely in the dark. I had to wear a glow stick around my neck—a glow stick that attracts bugs. These bugs were attacking my head and neck. I noticed everyone else was holding it in their hand. It wasn't until it was over that I realized they were doing that to keep from wasting energy swatting bugs off their head.

Because I drank a water bottle between every aid station, I'd find a telephone pole about a mile later to relieve myself. At mile twenty-three my time was thirteen hours and seven minutes. I had almost an hour to cover three miles and make it to the skylights visible across the lake. I decided to walk to guarantee my finish. I wanted that finisher's medal.

Then I started thinking about not finishing. I wondered if I was getting lightheaded. After all, I had gotten up at 4:30 a.m. and gone for a very long swim and very long bike ride, and then very long run. I thought it would be horrible to make it this far and not finish. I didn't know if I would ever train that hard and long again. I wondered what my wife and kids would say if I didn't finish. I considered finding a place to sit down and calm down. I was sleepy. I just wanted a nap . . . I wanted to turn on the television, lie down in bed, and go to sleep.

I'd never prepared for being sleepy tired during the event. I really thought I should lie down for a minute and rest. After all, I was way under my goal. This way, I thought, I could guarantee my finish.

I thought about my friend Carol, who had told me about her first ironman experience, how she had gotten tired at mile twenty-three and she took off running and ran through it.

Part of me wanted to lie down and part of me wanted to take off. I ran. I told myself, 'Get to the finish before you can't make it.' I caught up to someone staggering and learned he still had another lap to go. He was planning on finishing. The positive bug bit me again.

I felt good, and at that late stage berated myself for not going faster, not pushing harder. I started thinking about training harder next time and going faster. I started thinking all those things you think when you can smell the finish line.

Then I even got a little cocky. I didn't want anyone to pass me. I wanted to make them earn it. After almost 140 miles of a controlled pace, that was kinda stupid.

At mile twenty-five—the Mad Dog tent—I had more chicken soup. 'This is it,' I said to myself. 'I'm just running now. I'm running all out and whatever happens, happens.'

When I turned off the lake—it must be half a mile away from

the finish—I left the pitch-black street and entered downtown where all the trees were lit with white Christmas lights. It was this beautiful bright atmosphere. Hairs were standing up on my arms because I knew, now, I was going to finish. After the last turn the street was barricaded, with people behind them who were all having a good time. I could see the finish line. A smile spread across my face and I heard the announcer call my name. I couldn't help sprinting across the finish line, even though I knew my legs would pay for it later. I always want to look good for the finish.

Nothing is like it. I crossed the finish line. I made it.

There were so many things I realized psychologically, philosophically when I finished. Before, I wondered why I did triathlons: for me, my wife, my kids, my peers? I think ironman was the first place I realized I had better be doing it for myself. Other people may act like they care, but they don't. But finishing an ironman is something I'll carry in my heart for the rest of my life that nobody can take away from me. It's like a degree.

I've also discovered that triathlons are not about swimming, biking, or running. They're about fitness. This is a different level of fitness. It's like they say about Mark Allen—he's said to be the fittest man in the world. He is an ironman. And so am I.

Kevin is a civilian mechanical engineer working for the U.S. Navy in Panama City, Florida. His friend Morrie finished the race in 13:28:36.

NEVER SAY NEVER AGAIN

JANE FRATESI

DATE OF BIRTH: OCTOBER 24, 1962

RACE: IRONMAN CANADA 1998

TIME: 15:12:39

My alarm was set for 4:30 A.M., but I awoke at 4:15. *Is this what it feels like when you know you're going to prison?* Dread. The day had arrived. And yet I voluntarily signed up for this. *I'm scared.* I didn't even know if I could finish. *My bike could fall apart beyond repair and I'd have to DNF. I might not be able to go to the bathroom before the race. What if my blood sugar gets so screwed up that I get sick and end up lying beside the road, puking my guts out? My quads or calves might cramp horribly. What if I have a two-hour swim?*

I chewed on a bagel with cream cheese then went down to the transition to get body-marked. I checked my bike and pumped the tires. With time to spare I placed inspirational messages in my friends' bike-run transition bags. Back in my hotel room I squeezed into my own wet suit. I was almost out the door when I realized I was forgetting to take my cycling bottles (one bottle frozen Ensure Plus, two bottles frozen Gatorade, one bottle Diet Coke, one bottle ice water to put in Jetstream).

Time flew by. It was like a wedding. It starts and then, boom, it's over and you think, 'Where did the time go?' That's what it was like getting ready for the race. I got up and I thought I had all this time and then suddenly it was time to get in the water.

Standing on the beach, ready for a warm-up swim, I realized I was still wearing shoes. I scanned the crowd for Robert, my husband, and Mike, my coach. Instead I saw Chris's wife, Tanya. She got my shoes, whether she wanted them or not. "Give these to Robert if you can," I said as I headed for the water.

The water in Okanagan Lake felt good and it helped calm my nerves. I found my friends from the TriDRS listserv: Gerry, Jay, Jason, and others. They were why I was at the starting line. In 1997 a bunch of my listserv friends did Ironman Canada and they posted race reports. They talked about how great Penticton was and a lot of people on the list started signing up. It snowballed. And I thought, shoot, if that person can do it, I can do it, so I registered online—less than four months after doing my first triathlon, a sprint-distance race.

We were in back when the cannon blew. We strolled into the water, laughing and talking. Finally I started swimming. *Here I go. My first ironman.*

Swimming was easy. I exerted little effort and felt like I was being pulled in a current, because I was—the draft of seventeen hundred other swimmers. The swim was slow and uneventful, until it was time to get out and I found myself stumbling on enormous rocks, flailing my arms, and doing a jerky balancing act to keep from falling over. I hit my watch: 1:22.

Once out of the lake I fell to the ground to allow the wet-suit strippers to do their job. I jumped up and felt disoriented. I got my transition bag, went to the changing tent, and plopped on a chair. There weren't very many people in there. I dumped all the stuff out of my bag and a volunteer tried to pick it up, thinking it was trash and dirty clothes. "No! I'm using this stuff!" I wiped off with moist towelettes. Munched on Pringles. Put on my cycling clothes. Weaved the heart-rate monitor through my heart-rate-monitor bra. Applied suntan lotion. Brushed my hair and put it into a ponytail. I was working on a twenty-minute transition.

I entered the bike transition area and was shocked to see what looked like about six bikes left. I had no problem finding my bike. It was the only one in my row. It was the only one in the area. I was truly at the back of the pack, but I tried not to let it bother me. As I left the transition, the commentator announced that my friend Jason was leaving the transition. As I pulled away, the last thing I heard was, ". . . and he lists his occupation as Jell-O wrestler."

I caught up to Jason and we chatted a while, but I began to worry about a blocking penalty. So I pulled ahead a little. My head started to hurt and I felt nauseous. The headache gradually worsened and I blamed it on my glasses. Maybe too much sugar. I don't know. I tried to drink the Ensure, but it was still frozen solid. I kept drinking water. The headache was pretty bad. I drank the Diet Coke and took three Tylenol.

At mile twenty-six I saw Mike and Robert and took the opportunity to stop and adjust my glasses in hopes of relieving my headache. Mike informed me I was three hours into the race, which surprised me. I screwed up my watch coming out of the transition and could only judge my race time by the time of day, which was set to Atlanta time, which is three hours ahead. This was a lot of math for a tired brain.

My food was unappealing. Gatorade: nauseating. Sugar: nauseating. I managed to eat a granola bar and drink Ensure. I tossed out one full bottle of Gatorade at an aid station in favor of water.

I passed my friend John from Atlanta, someone I knew from

my triathlon club. He looked hot and uncomfortable. Sweat was pouring from his face straight down on his legs. It was hot. "Hey John," I said as I passed. "Hey," he said, looking sideways at me. *Oh man, he looks really bad.* I felt sorry for him. *Wow, I could actually feel a lot worse than I feel now.* He was proof I didn't feel as bad as I could.

I took on Richter Pass, a large winding climb about forty miles into the ride. I had trained on the hills in Georgia, so it didn't seem that bad to me. I passed a lot of folks and road graffiti on the way up.

At mile sixty-five my front tire went flat. I had no idea why. I dismounted, removed the wheel and stood the bike up on its fork. As I picked up the wheel, the bike fell, dumping water from my Jetstream and busting open my remaining bottle of Gatorade. *Good riddance.* I sat on the ground, removed the old tube, and replaced it with a new one. *I can do this.* I had never changed a flat, only seen it done by others in my riding group. As I thought about what to do next, a pickup truck from the Bike Barn, the local bike store, stopped across the street. A guy hopped out and ran toward me with a floor pump. *Yes!* He instructed me to sit there and eat while he fixed my flat. I munched on cinnamon graham crackers and within a few minutes the flat was fixed. *Thank you, Bike Barn.*

Finally I got to the special-needs bags. I stopped and examined the contents, all of which I had packed the night before. What I thought would be appealing was all nauseating, except the Apple Newtons. I removed the Newtons and extra headband. I applied more suntan lotion. I tossed the remains—a Power Bar, Pringles, and more Gatorade.

Robert and Mike were a few miles up the road. I stopped to give them a report and, while I was off my bike, I went to pee behind the bushes. "I know what you're doing back there!"

yelled a cyclist as he passed.

Near mile ninety I got to Yellow Lake, along which is a grad-
ual climb that is ultimately much steeper than Richter Pass. I
saw people walking and pushing their bikes uphill. *Man I must
really be at the back of the pack. I* will not *push my bike up this hill.
I've done steeper, longer climbs, in hotter weather, higher humidity,
when I was more tired than this.* Still, the climb was surprisingly
difficult. My legs really hurt. *I will not walk.* My speed was five
miles per hour. I knew I could go two miles per hour without
falling over. *Ugh! Why is this so hard? Why does this hurt so much?
Crank. Crank. Crank. I'm sick of this crap! I want this damn ride to
be over.* I had gone from feeling great to feeling demoralized and
defeated in a matter of minutes. Finally I reached the top and
tried to throw my chain onto the big chain ring, but realized it
was already there. *Aaaaaaa! I can't believe I climbed that whole
damn thing in the big chain ring!* For reasons still unknown to me,
I immediately switched to the small chain ring (my best guess
was to make up for climbing in the big ring) and threw the
chain completely off. It was too far off to get back on without
stopping. As I dismounted, I hit my behind-the-seat bottle carrier as I swung my leg around, dragging my bike to the ground.
All fluids dumped out. I picked up the bike and fixed the chain.
I swung my leg back over to get on, but my leg just wouldn't go
as high as my brain told it to and I hit the bottle carrier again,
knocking the bike to the ground. I tried to lift my leg over the
top tube, but instead kicked the top tube, again knocking my
bike to the ground. I stood there looking out over Yellow Lake,
which is beautifully set in a valley with mountains rising in all
directions. I couldn't enjoy the scenery. Instead, I imagined how
wonderful it would feel to hurl my bike into the lake and spew
obscenities that would echo off the mountains. Somehow it happened that I got back on my bike, demoralized, depressed, and

generally pissed.

After Yellow Lake there was still one more hill. Everyone talks about Yellow Lake so when you get to the top you think, 'I have no more climbing to do, that's it.' But it's not. There's one more hill. And when you're that tired it looks like a huge hill. And at that point I just wanted to cry.

The wind was so strong it was hard to get up any real speed going downhill into town. Nothing near the fifty-five miles per hour people bragged about from years past.

Finally I hit Main Street, heading toward the transition. Main Street is pancake flat, but the headwinds were incredible. I kept switching into easier gears but I could only maintain a speed of twelve miles per hour. It was less than five miles to the finish but it seemed like it would never end. I felt like I was crawling in slow motion. As I approached the transition area, the fifth-place man was finishing. I entered the transition area and rode through to the back, as I passed what seemed like all seventeen hundred bikes already parked in the transition.

Volunteers grabbed my bike and held it upright to help me get off. I knew from previous experience this wasn't going to work. I stood there, straddling my top tube. "I can't get off my bike," I said to my helpers. They tilted it to the side so that it reached a level I could lift my leg over.

I had another twenty-minute transition. I walked leisurely to the changing tent. The air in the tent was one hundred degrees warmer than the air outside. There were more volunteers in the tent than athletes. I plopped on a chair, dumped out the bag and sifted through my stuff. I ate more Pringles but I was losing my appetite for everything. I removed the sweaty, salty cycling clothes. Wiped arms, legs, and face with moist towelettes. I didn't want to start the run sweaty. Reapplied sunscreen. Brushed my hair and put it back in a ponytail. Put on my clothes. Shoes.

Hat. Race Belt. Lots of Vaseline.

I left the tent and headed to a Porta-Potti. As I sat there I heard the lead female, Lori Bowden, finish. *Oh my God she's finished and I'm not even on the run course yet.*

I walked to the run start and began jogging. *Ouch. Ouch. Ouch.* I hadn't seen a cloud all day. I knew Robert and Mike would be out there and I didn't want them to see me walk. I jogged until I saw them, waved, and kept jogging until I hit the first aid station. I ate watermelon. I ate and drank too much, but the watermelon tasted so good. I took two salt tablets. I had no real motivation to run. *Walking feels just fine.* After a while, walking got boring, so I ran. I was able to maintain a good pace. My plan was to walk up every hill and through every aid station, but run the rest. I enjoyed the cheers of spectators and was amazed that so many people came out to sit in their front yards in the heat. Some of them looked up my name in the roster and called out "Go Jane" or "Go Jane from Atlanta." I thanked each one of them as I passed.

I ran with a girl named Jennifer for a while. She complained of feeling "barfy." We had something in common. It was her first ironman, too. "I knew this would be difficult," she said. "But I didn't know I'd feel so bad."

I'm glad I wore my TriDRS singlet. Many people recognized me and called my name as they passed going the other way. I would not have recognized most of them otherwise. Finally the chicken broth hit the aid stations. I had lost my tolerance for solid food many hours ago, and all sugar was repulsive, so the broth was a big treat. Salty and hot. I temporarily abandoned my vegetarianism and drank the chicken broth at every aid station from mile six on. It was the only thing keeping me alive.

Very few people were running. The farther into the course I got, the fewer runners I saw. At many points everyone in sight was walking in silence. Heads low. Plodding along. Just trying to make it to the next aid station. Fortunately, the sun was rapidly sinking behind the mountains. Although I never really set a time goal, I had delusions of finishing before dark, but now I just thought about getting to the run halfway point before dark. I did.

I ran with Ron for a while. It was nice to have someone to run-walk with and talk to. I started to pass people I saw on the way to the turnaround and realized I was moving at a decent pace. Darkness fell near mile fifteen.

Mile eighteen I was really starting to feel the fatigue, although I was still running quite a bit. I continued walking the hills, walking the aid stations, and drinking chicken soup. It was wonderful having Robert and Mike out on the course. Sometimes they rode beside me in silence, sometimes they rode on ahead, sometimes they walked with me through the aid stations. Always, they told me I looked strong. Somehow I ended up at mile twenty-three.

I couldn't predict my finishing time. I didn't really know how far I was into the race, because I only had Atlanta time to go by. By mile twenty-four I decided that I'd come in just after fifteen hours or just after sixteen hours. I wasn't sure.

I saw the marker for mile twenty-five. What a beautiful sign. Nothing could stop me. If every muscle in my legs cramped I could still drag myself on my elbows for 1.2 miles.

As I ran down Main Street, by the Hog's Breath Café, it was lined with people and they started closing in. They were cheering and high-fiving me. I liked high-fiving the kids, but the older guys slapped my hand so hard it threw my arm back. I was so tired and so scared I was going to get knocked over. I rounded the corner to the finish and people were cheering. I ran as fast as I comfortably could.

I crossed the finish line in 15:12:39. My run time was 5:39. I didn't feel elated—more relieved it was over. I had never imagined a spectacular finish. Now I could say I had done an ironman, and there was no way I was going to train next year because it had killed me that year. When people told me the training is much harder than the race, they were dead right. I am not training for an ironman next year. No way.

Jane did go back to Canada the next year and then competed in Ironman New Zealand six months later.

A DECADE OF DREAMING

RICK OLSON

DATE OF BIRTH: AUGUST 31, 1956

RACE: HAWAII IRONMAN 1999

TIME: 12:49:43

I've had two great days in my life. One was floating down a river in Jamaica, relaxing while I drank Red Stripe. The other was in Kona, floating on pure determination to get myself to the finish of the Hawaii Ironman. I still get chills thinking about it.

On race day I was hardly nervous. I was a player in a major spectacle of epic proportions. I didn't know how it was going to unfold. I was there, participating, and it was like living a dream. A dream I had envisioned for ten years.

I had finally arrived. In 1988, after having run two marathons I was looking for more of a challenge so I entered a triathlon. As soon as I did my first sprint race everyone started asking, "Have you done the Ironman?" They didn't know about any other triathlon. After my first exposure to triathlon I knew I would have to do it. I sent away for a lottery slot in 1989. Then again and again. I entered the lottery seven times in ten years and always got a rejection letter. Actually, I knew my fate before getting the letter because I was impatient and always called the race office to hear the news. It was always the same. "Sorry." I'd go from this feeling of hope and great expectation to a sinking feeling that started in my throat and settled in the pit of my stomach. I thought I'd never get in. It wasn't in my control, so all I could do was keep entering and hoping maybe . . . the big maybe.

I didn't consider doing another ironman-distance race. I figured I'd only want to do one ironman in my lifetime so Hawaii had to be it. Hawaii is where it all started. It had the magic for me. I planned to do one and get it out of my system, hate it and never do another thing like that again. I had to shoot for Hawaii. Luckily there was a lottery system for pokies like me, the people who don't train all year round.

When I received the word—Yes, I was in—it couldn't have come at a worse time. I was overweight, I hadn't run in months, hadn't competed in a triathlon in years. Suddenly I had a reason to train again.

Unlike a lot of triathletes, triathlon training is not a lifestyle for me. See, I don't like training. The ironman is the only thing I've ever trained for. Even the marathons I've done, I only did an eight- or ten-mile run and then went out and did it. Training is okay, but I like racing a lot better. There's a different dynamic to it. Ironman is the only thing I put time into because that was the only event that ever scared me. Plus, training for ironman is more like being on a journey. And in this case the journey is the reward.

The water was beautiful, just as I imagined it would be, warm and inviting. I enjoyed interacting with the other racers near me and when a helicopter flew over us, I remembered again that I was part of something special. It was such an honor to be there. I can only hope to do it again.

I had heard the swim would be frantic but I thought it was pretty easy to get out of the harbor. As I swam to the glass-bottomed boat marking the turnaround, I wondered how I would assemble three sports together in one day. I had worked my training up to a 110-mile ride, one 22-mile run, and one 3-mile swim. It would be interesting to see how my body responded. Cruise the course, I told myself. Have fun. When I reached the boat I waved to the people watching and asked for French toast.

The one worry I couldn't shake was that my bike would break down. Even if my body was a wreck, I knew I'd finish. The swim was only ten percent of my day. The bike, though, that would set me up for the run. My main focus was to conserve and finish.

Up Pay and Save Hill to the Queen K, I absorbed all the sights and sounds—I was particularly conscious of other participants around me. It was tight up that hill—one wrong move could put a damper on the rest of the day. I was riding defensively—I didn't want to wreck. I didn't want to walk away from my one chance to do this race.

Once out on the course, wow, it was such a bitchin' ride. I don't like wind, but I like the winds out there. They are a living entity—they flow around you. It was magical.

Ironman officials run quality races in part because the race volunteers treat the athletes like royalty. It was kind of odd for me, but it's something I marvel at. Sure it's a long distance, but you're treated like gold and they'll do anything for you. Volunteers ran alongside me and enthusiastically passed me stuff. The precision—it's like a machine. At the bike turn in Hawi—it's a little town but everyone was out there cheering—I was treated like gold. Volunteers did everything but ride and run the race for me.

On the way back to town I was kind of wishing they would. It got really hard coming back—not as bad as it could be—but there was always a headwind. It helped that there was cloud cover that year, which cooled things off considerably.

Finishing the ride is a sensory festival after being on the Queen K so long. There were stimuli everywhere and my adrenaline was pumped up. Right before the Kona Surf that last hill is pretty steep. With all the spectators there I forgot it was coming. All of a sudden there was a pretty sharp grade. It drained any last energy I had and made me think I didn't have anything left for the marathon. That was humbling.

I realized that ironman is about monitoring all parts of the body at all times because things change so quickly out there. I could go from feeling great to feeling like complete dog doo to feeling great again, sometimes within a span of thirty minutes.

In general, I tend to be fairly decent on the swim and bike, and it always comes down to the run. "Jeez, it's going to be long," I lamented when I got off the bike. I wanted to get to the Queen K as fast as I could to be alone. A lot of people crowded Alii Drive and I felt beholden to them to run and feel good. They were cheering me on but I was dog-tired. "Rick Olson, get your butt in gear," they'd yell after looking up my name in the program. I was so ready to do my own thing.

My feet felt like someone had hammered them with a meat cleaver. They were very tender. I had poured water over my head several times throughout the bike and as my feet got wet it formed the perfect environment for blisters. It was a long way to the finish. The marathon is where the rubber meets the road. Everything else seems so easy by comparison.

Just past town I saw my wife, who tried to get me to pose for a picture. I wasn't exactly up for it. I had my race face on. Didn't want to walk. I tried to stay cool. Even with the cloud cover it still was hot and humid—it was like an oven. I piled ice on my head at every aid station.

When I finally got to the Queen K, I felt sick—violently sick.

My stomach felt like crap. There was nothing I wanted to eat. Absolutely no more GUs. I survived the last twelve miles on chicken broth.

It was a junkyard out in the Energy Lab. All these people, with all these dreams, lying on the side of the road moaning. I could feel their pain too and there was nothing I could do about it. I saw someone vomiting and thought that could be me in half an hour, or five minutes. I wondered how hard I could push without totaling myself. All of us were pushing through barriers. There was a lot of inspiration out there.

As I got back on the highway I saw more disoriented people heading toward the turnaround. "How much farther?" they'd ask. I was just there, but I didn't know the answer. Everyone had this partial look of dazed terror.

Back in town I woke up. Oh yeah, I'm finishing the Ironman! The crowds bolstered my performance quite a bit. I rounded the hot corner and felt electrified. It was like being on stage at a rock concert. I ran through a tunnel of sound, finally, to my appointed destination. I was running on the hallowed ground of Dave Scott and Mark Allen. All of a sudden the hardship was gone—I could have run a couple of more miles on the rush of emotion. It doesn't get any better. If I could relive one day in my life, that would be it.

When Rick's neighbors started asking if he would do Ironman California—a race practically in his backyard—once again he felt the pressure to sign up, and despite a bout with the flu, he finished in fifteen hours. He also plans to do Ironman Canada, and dreams of going back to Hawaii. So much for the 'I just need to get this out of my system' theory.

TOO CLOSE FOR COMFORT

Finishers cross the line with less than an hour to spare.

THE BRIDE WORE A FINISHER'S SHIRT

LUCIE MARTIN

DATE OF BIRTH: MAY 26, 1967

RACE: IRONMAN USA 2000

TIME: 16:30:52

My first ironman started at a drunken dinner at Langans restaurant in London. Six of us gathered to wish our friends Tim and Lizzy bon voyage as they headed to the United States for Tim to earn his MBA at Tuck University.

Tim and my partner, Brian, had completed ironmans before—Brian four times—and as we were all members of East London Triathletes, the conversation inevitably turned to racing.

Tim and Lizzy were recently married and the usual "your turn next" comments cropped up. Brian made a crack that he'd marry me if I completed the ironman. I could only roll my eyes. "If I did complete it, it would be for my own personal satisfaction," I retorted. "Certainly not a condition of marriage!"

Tim and Lizzy informed the group there was an ironman event in Lake Placid, fairly close to where they were going to live. "Wouldn't it be cool if we all went and did it?" Tim piped up. The other couple, also named Tim and Elizabeth, agreed. Then Lizzy added, "You and Brian could get married out there as well." With that, the deal was done and the die was cast. The three couples signed up on the Internet.

Although the proposal was tongue in cheek—and somewhat backhanded—that was as close as he got and as much as we discussed it. But I took him on his word and began wedding preparations as soon as our race entries were confirmed.

Long months of winter and spring training followed. We had a fairly mild winter, although there were some long, wet rides. There were many times when we wondered what on earth had possessed us to agree to this, but no one wanted to back out.

Least of all me. Lizzy, in New Hampshire now, found a house for us to rent with a beautiful garden Brian and I could marry in. She found a JP and hired a florist.

July dawned and before we knew it we were all off to America. We spent the first week in New Hampshire, just getting used to the time difference and chilling out. We arrived in Lake Placid on Friday and on Saturday our guests arrived—my parents, Brian's parents, more family, and three other couples. There were twenty of us in total.

Our parents weren't told about the wedding plans. As far as they were concerned, we had paid their way to watch the race as anniversary presents to them—my parents' fiftieth and Brian's parents' fortieth. When they showed up we told them, "By the way, we're getting married on Wednesday." But my mum, she had rumbled me. She had brought a card and confetti. She's not daft.

In a way the wedding detracted from the stress of the race. It gave me something else to think about. The six of us racing are all close friends, but there was a lot of tension. We cope with stress in different ways. My way of coping is not to think about it. I knew more training wasn't going to make me fitter, it was just going to tire me and injure me. It was inevitable that race day would come. It also was going to pass. And one way or another I was going to be spat out the back of this. There was nothing to do about it but flow through it. My friends examined race preparation and planning in meticulous detail. I found it difficult to be in their company when they were scanning the race information for the one hundredth time or studying course maps, because it would stress me out big time. The wedding helped keep my mind off it.

To an extent, that is, because I still have never been so scared in all my life. I was absolutely petrified about the swim and I looked at that lake with dread. For some reason I thought I was going to die. I was paranoid and had a bad feeling about it. We had visited Lake Placid in March—a reconnaissance trip for the wedding and the race—when it was ten degrees below zero and snow everywhere. There was sixteen inches of ice on Mirror Lake—we went dogsledding on it. This thought stayed with me because I can't cope with cold water.

Race registration was a nightmare. We were handed a questionnaire to complete about how much training we had done and our nutrition during training. Although we had had a coach schedule our sessions for us, those questions completely freaked me out and led me to believe that in no way had I done enough, and there was no way I was going to get 'round. When I got to the desk to collect my race numbers and transition bags, the guy took one look at me, picked up the Hawaii qualification form and said sarcastically, "Be needing this, do you think?" With that I left in tears.

Brian, the iron veteran, was having problems of his own. Late on Friday night—after midnight—our phone rang and Brian had leapt out of bed to answer it. It was my sister calling. She had had a complete nightmare flight from the UK and was stuck in Newark. But Brian had tossed the phone to me, writhing in pain, because he had stubbed his toe and broke it. Two days before the race—it was a complete disaster—but he carried on to finish, albeit an hour slower than his usual time.

I thought I was going to be sick on race morning. The lake was fogbound and I couldn't see the first buoy. Lizzy and I had already planned to buddy up on the swim so we got in together and held back. I stood there with Lizzy whilst a woman sang the American national anthem. Another American triathlete was next to us and cried her eyes out. It was her first time too and all three of us ended up hugging and crying. There was no warning before the gun went off. Suddenly it was time to move.

Despite my anxiety, the swim went really well. I came out smack bang on one hour thirty like I had hoped. Lizzy and I stayed together and exited the water together. Elizabeth wasn't far behind us and we all met up in transition and had another cry.

I had huge problems on the bike, which surprised me because I had been quite confident about this leg. I had put the miles in, but I got on that bike and died within the first ten miles. The first climb—which comes early in the ride—I had no power in my legs. Up the same climb on the second lap I knew I was in trouble. I got off at sixty miles and sat by the road taking fluids and eating a Clif Bar. I wasn't going to give up, I simply needed to regroup. An ambulance pulled over to check on my condition. With that I forced myself to continue. The last forty miles I realized I was cutting it close and was concerned I wouldn't make it back. I kept checking my watch and looking at my speed, aware that I had to be back by 5:30 in the afternoon. I was very anxious about making that bike cutoff, but in the end I made it by thirty minutes. I was so relieved I treated myself to a neck massage in transition. I knew I was going to finish. It would be a bad time but nothing was going to stop me now.

I set off on the marathon and saw Brian already on his second run lap. He was suffering with his broken toe, but he spurred me to carry on.

Our cheering section/wedding guests were out waving Union Jacks. Dad was concerned for me—he knew my anticipated time was fourteen hours and I was way off the mark. When I started the run he wouldn't leave for lunch until I came through on the first lap. My family had to bring him a doggie bag. When I came by he was so relieved.

"Where you been? How are you? You feeling okay?"

"Well I've had better days, Dad."

"You're not in distress?"

"No, I'm not in distress, I'm going to carry on."

I eventually caught Lizzy at nineteen miles and we were both spent. "Ah stuff this, we're going to walk," we agreed and set off cursing that dinner party.

As we got closer to the stadium there was a little downhill stretch, I told Lizzie, "We're not going to walk into the stadium, were going to run into the stadium." The crowd just erupted when we arrived. As we came into the finishing straight, Brian called out my name and handed me the Cross of St. George, the English part of the British flag. Lizzy and I crossed the line together in sixteen hours and thirty minutes, half an hour short of the cutoff time. I ran in, flag waving, then collapsed in Brian's arms. "Well done," he said. My knees went as he held on to me. "Medic!" he yelled.

After the race I spent two hours in the medical tent. I was hypothermic with a body temperature of ninety-three degrees. I was also dehydrated and got three litres of saline IV, but no massage; it was too late for that.

I had three days to recover and transition from ironman to bride. Apart from being stiff and sore, I had worn a short-sleeved cycling jersey and was sunburned from the middle of my arm down, and I had a bloody sleeveless wedding dress. There was not enough time to top it off with a tan. I thought, my "something borrowed" would solve the problem—it was a pair of long silk gloves. Long enough, I hoped, to cover my sunburn. But the lovely gloves stopped short, just two inches below the sunburn, and then white arm. I thought it was best to hold them instead of wear them. It's very noticeable in our wedding photos, as is Brian's black eye from the kick in the face he received during the swim. In the end we knew it was all going to be something to laugh at later.

In fact it came with the territory. This was a whole package, ironman and wedding. There was never any distinction between the two. I almost didn't think too much about the details of the wedding until after the race. The morning of the wedding I felt very nervous—even more so when the JP turned up to marry us. I walked out into the garden with my dad and I had no idea how the ceremony was going to run because we hadn't rehearsed. I didn't know what I was expected to say and when. There was no training for this!

It turned out none was needed. The ceremony couldn't have gone off any better. After, we all sat down to a wedding buffet cooked by Tim and Elizabeth. It was a perfect day.

I feel married, but I still don't feel like an ironman. It's so hard to believe. I feel a bit of a fraud because I did such a bad time. But I am an ironman. I made that midnight cutoff.

Although I had promised my family I would never do another one, I've decided I'd like to mark my fortieth birthday with an ironman finish. I haven't decided on a venue, but I quite fancy California.

Lucie, an insurance assessor in London, made her finish more "real" by getting a tattoo as a constant reminder of her ironman status. It's a red ironman emblem on the top of her right thigh.

AIN'T NO MOUNTAIN HIGHER

PATRICK CONNOR

DATE OF BIRTH: MARCH 30, 1960

RACE: IRONMAN NEW ZEALAND 1998

TIME: 15:16:41

Ironman is like mountain climbing. On a mountain you take one step at a time and take what the day gives you—if it's one-hundred-mile-per-hour winds, if it's subzero temperature, if it's dehydration. And really that's what ironman is all about too. Whether it's wind and rain, extreme hot or cold, mechanical problems or nutrition problems, you have to stay in the moment to get through it, as opposed to looking ahead and becoming overwhelmed because you still have four thousand vertical feet to go or sixty miles on the bike and a 26.2-mile run.

I started doing triathlons because I stopped mountain climbing. I got the ultimate climbing experience while on Mount Rainier during a winter expedition to train for Mount McKinley the following May. We experienced terrible weather. Fifteen inches of snow a day, thirty-five-mile-per-hour wind, and temperatures clinging to thirty degrees below zero with the wind-chill factor. We climbed as much as we could, but couldn't quite make the summit. We left at ten thousand feet, and on the way down the storm got worse. With seven-foot visibility, getting knocked down constantly by one-hundred-mile-per-hour gusts, and an hour away from sunset, we had to bivouac. We dug two snow caves at seventy-five-hundred feet and spent the night tucked away like hibernating bears. That experience, with superficial frostbite that took two painful weeks to heal, was enough to get me off the mountain. Something didn't feel right about McKinley. My girlfriend at the time, who had been on the mountain with me, asked, "Why don't we do triathlons?"

I took two weeks of swim lessons, borrowed a bike from her, and did my first triathlon. I was addicted from there. I sucked at it, but I was hungry to get better. I did two more and decided I wanted to do an ironman-distance race. I registered for Ironman New Zealand that September. It was the last year the race was held in Auckland.

Race morning felt like getting to the top of a hill on a roller coaster. I was nervous, but I was excited too. It was probably helpful that I didn't know what I was getting myself into. I was naive that morning, like I had been about my training. I didn't know that seventy-mile training rides weren't long enough. I didn't know what a brick was. I didn't know what to eat or put in a special-needs bag. But on that morning ignorance was bliss. I have friends now who do their first ironman and they think about it too much and end up afraid of it. When race morning came around for me, I was eager to jump in—despite the weather.

It was an El Niño year and the race started during a storm. It appeared the sea and sky had traded places that morning. I puked three times in St. Helier's Bay. No matter which way I turned my head to breathe, I swallowed water. After spending an hour and twenty-three minutes in the bay, I changed 'costumes' and got on the bike to experience all sorts of microclimates. One moment it was damp and drizzly; the next moment it was sunny. I pressed forward eager to see what the next few miles would bring me. It was like getting to the next chapter of a good book.

The terrain reminded me of San Francisco, with its hills and valleys. At one point we had an ocean view. I hit the turnaround in 3:15, well within my goal time. It was nice while it lasted. Six miles later, while winding up a technical climb, the sun disappeared and it started to pour again. On my way down the corkscrew, cruising at about twenty-five miles-an-hour with more brake than I should have, I started to hydroplane. The roads weren't closed to traffic. My choices were the stone face of a mountain, oncoming traffic, or, worse yet, going over the cliff. Before I got to select my poison, my bike slid out from under me. I cracked the back of my helmet when I hit the pavement, my handlebars were bent slightly, my computer was crushed and gone, and my rear wheel was bent so bad that it rubbed against the frame. The only way I could make it spin was to totally release the rear brake and even then it rubbed. My jersey was torn. I had road rash all along the left side of my body. This was what the day gave me. Quitting was not an option. I'd be damned if I was going to travel this far and not finish. It was like spending thirteen hours in a snow cave. At this point what I'd need to make it through was perseverance. I knew I had that in me. I had seen it at work just a little more than a year ago. So I spent ten minutes doing what I could to repair my bike before I carried on.

With my tire knocking my frame on each stroke, I had to put in more effort to pedal. The microclimates continued their kaleidoscope of seasons before me. I continued on through a hailstorm, then heat, then more rain. My back ached and I stopped frequently to stretch, while keeping an eye on my watch. I knew I had eight and a half hours to make the transition. Cutoff for the race was fifteen and a half hours. It would be close for both.

I spent fifteen minutes in the transition, changing clothes again, tending to my cuts, and wishing I could get a massage. But I learned I would need a doctor's approval to get one as well as permission to continue the race if I had one. Screw that.

The run turned out to be the easiest part of my day, despite the banging headwind. I met up with one of my friends early on, which was good and bad. I was trying to motivate and move Jennifer along. She was getting pissed off at me because she was afraid I was not going to finish because of her. I couldn't convince her I wasn't worried about it. Even though it was close, I was confident we were going to finish.

The run started with a three-mile out-and-back of hilly terrain then flattened out along St. Helier's Bay to the downtown area and back. The course consisted of the out-and-back, then two ten-mile loops. The rain finally ceased. It was merely dark and cold.

I gave up on Jennifer near twenty miles. It was tough, because with six miles to go she was crying, but she implored me to go on, worried she was holding me back.

I knew I was going to make it because I had seen it happen the day before. I watched race organizers as they constructed the finish line, which was built on a wooden stage. I stood in front of it, then walked across the finish, visualizing what it would be like for me. When I was coming down the road, I heard the announcer call my name amid the "Good on ya mate!" and "Well done!" from the crowds. They were wild and thumping on the stage as each finisher approached. My friends supporting me there were phenomenal. I made the finish cutoff by fourteen minutes. Jennifer squeezed in with seven minutes left.

Even though I hadn't been a triathlete very long and didn't

know much about what I was getting into before the race, I had a very good sense for what I had accomplished not only in sheer distance but also in what it took to get through that day. My emotions reminded me of every second, every inch of the course, as I crossed the finish line. It was tougher than I ever expected it would be. The idea of climbing Mount McKinley didn't seem so bad anymore.

After arriving home from New Zealand, Patrick got a coach and finished Ironman Florida 1999 (11:11) and Ironman California 2000 (12:08). Two weeks before his Ironman California race Patrick was diagnosed with lymphoma. He applied his principles for mountain climbing and ironman racing to chemotherapy and is currently in remission. He plans to race Ironman Africa and Ironman California next.

ANGELS SEEN AND UNSEEN

TERRY JORDAN

DATE OF BIRTH: OCTOBER 17, 1957

RACE: IRONMAN USA 1999

TIME: 16:57:44

Terry Jordan's husband, Bob, was featured on NBC's coverage of the 1997 Hawaii Ironman. He was competing because their five-year-old daughter, Emily, had written a letter asking the World Triathlon Corporation to give her dad an Ironman slot for his birthday. Emily died of leukemia five days after he received the slot, but her spirit lives on in many ironman athletes, including her mom.

I woke up at 4:20 A.M. and got moving right away. I showered, put on my bathing suit and some real clothes—jeans and a TEAM-IN-TRAINING sweatshirt. I gathered my wet suit, goggles, and journal, as well as clothes for after the race. After the race. It seemed so far away.

I drank my coffee, some orange juice, and ate a small bowl of raisin bran. Then it was time to ready my mind. I read my meditation book, lit a candle, and said a prayer. It was the twenty-third anniversary of my dad's death. I also reflected on the memory of my daughter, Emily. Last year I learned that a thirty-member team for the Leukemia and Lymphoma Society's Team-in-Training wanted to do their race—Ironman Canada— in memory of Emily. When I learned that none of them had ever done an ironman before, it shocked me. At first I said, "I could never do that." And then I thought, 'Could I do that? Why not, what's in my way?' It had been nine years since I had done a triathlon before I began training for this. I was always iron support for my husband, Bob, while caring for Emily. Even though we had just moved across country and I was busy raising our toddler son, Timothy, those reasons weren't enough to stop me. The best excuse I could come up with was that we had just bought a comfy couch.

There was a lot to do at the race start. I got numbered, picked up timing chip, put water bottles on bike, filled Bento Box with PB&J bagel, pumped up tires, delivered special-needs bags, stood in potty line, checked out swim start, stood in potty line, put on wet suit halfway so I could stand in potty line one more time (finally, success). Now there was time to meditate and write in my journal.

At 6:45 A.M. I found Bob and Timothy and gave them my bag of stuff. A woman approached us and said, "Look! Bob Jordan's wife is doing this!" She sounded surprised. I guess I was too. There had to have been more than one hundred people who approached Bob or me during the week and said they had seen the 1997 NBC Hawaii Ironman documentary. People would see me and say, "That's Bob Jordan's wife."

So there I was, Bob Jordan's wife, ready to do what Bob had done many times before, including on national television in front of millions of viewers. I was grateful I wasn't being filmed. I kissed Bob and Timothy and headed to the beach, finding the table to put my glasses on before getting into the water.

Our first date in 1988 was the Bay State Triathlon in Massachusetts. Bob was racing and I was interested in getting into the sport. I watched him and loved it. I knew I wanted to do it too and entered some smaller races. In 1990 we did Bay State together and the next month we were married. After that, nothing. Because after that I became a mom. But still triathlon has been such a big part of our lives. Every vacation we went on for the first eight years of our marriage, including our honeymoon, revolved around triathlon. It was me watching Bob.

The gun went off at 7 A.M. and the clock began to roll. I found a place in the water where there were not too many others (as if) and kept a steady pace. I felt people all over my body. I found that if I stopped kicking and just pulled with my arms for a moment, I didn't kick anyone in the face and they quickly found a new place to swim. There was a cable that ran the entire swim course about six or seven feet under water. I found it and used it as a guide so I didn't need to pay attention to the buoys.

I absolutely loved the swim. The water felt wonderful and safe. The sun was rising and casting beautiful patterns through the air and down into the water. The view of fifteen hundred bodies all moving gracefully was amazing.

The swim was a double-loop course. We actually had to get out of the water, go under the starting gate, and start again for another 1.2-mile swim. After my first loop, I told the volunteers, "That swim was just so nice, I think I'll do it again!" And off I went.

I finished the swim in 1:24. Someone stripped off my wet suit and handed it to me. Then I saw Bob and Timothy and my cousins (Michael, Paula and their children Kerri, Kelly, and Kasey) and my aunt Mary. More kisses and high fives and I ran about half a mile from the beach and got into my bike clothes. Then I remembered my glasses! I told a volunteer and she said she would make sure they were in one of my bags.

I began riding the bike course that has been described as the most beautiful ironman course in the world and I didn't have my glasses on! No matter, what I *could* see was beautiful. Between my aerobars was a picture of Emily. I could see her smile just fine.

The course began with a nice descent into the town of Keene that went for about six to eight miles. The wind coming up the hill, which grew stronger as the day wore on, was a bit of a bummer. I could only get up to about thirty-nine miles per hour. I had heard that folks could reach up to sixty, but not on this day, at least not for me.

The course was very hilly. We had to climb up and up and up again, but the views were incredible (I think). Waterfalls, streams and rivers, rolling farms, and beautiful vistas.

I was about a mile from town ready to complete my first bike loop when Thomas Hellriegel (who eventually went on to win the race) came upon me on his second loop. He passed me and I came into town right behind him asking people, "Where is Thomas? Am I closing in on him?" People were howling and cheering me on.

'Another fifty-six miles and *then* a marathon lie between you and the finish line. Be strong, Terry Jordan! Be an ironman!' This was a line from the 1997 Ironman documentary in which I substituted my name for Bob's. It became my mantra. 'Be strong, Terry Jordan! Be an ironman!'

The wind really picked up on the second loop and I lost time. The main thing I focused on was getting lots of food into my body to prepare for the run. The bike was long and I didn't meet too many people who wanted to chat, so it was a bit lonely. I began to realize that I'm a socializer and that's what energizes me.

I made the bike cutoff with fifteen minutes to spare and got changed into my running clothes. It took me about fifteen minutes to change, pee, and drink some Coke (I never drink Coke, but I needed the caffeine as I missed my nap that day). Best of all, my glasses were in my bike-to-run bag! Now I would be able to see the run course, but unfortunately it would be pitch black.

It was 5:30 in the evening and I was beginning my very first marathon. I was thinking how great it was to be there, to be alive, to have been inspired by a team of folks in California, to have Bob and Timothy cheering me on along with my cousins and aunt, to have my dad and sweet Emily with me, as well as so much support and love from angels seen and unseen. I truly felt surrounded.

I see now that miracles happen. The loss of Emily broke my heart deeper than any heartbreak I have ever known. But it also made my heart expand. I discovered I was capable of enduring more pain, more joy, more sadness, more love. Losing her wasn't what I expected. Neither was doing an ironman. And that *is* a miracle.

The run was my biggest concern before the race, being uncharted territory. It turned out to be my favorite part because there were so many people to talk to. I felt so strong, so good, just keeping my slow and steady pace, kind of like a turtle. And if I saw someone who didn't look good, I stopped to see how they were doing.

One woman, Peggy, was ready to break down and cry. The tears began to flow when I stopped to walk with her. I asked what she was feeling and she said, "I can't go on. It's my stomach. I've never felt this before. I just can't continue."

I noticed she had a pierced eyebrow and figured she'd be open to some alternative suggestions for healing. I told her about hands, especially the palms and how healing they are. I made a suggestion that she imagine breathing in the healing energy of the nature around us and place her palm over her abdomen. Next I suggested that she breathe out to imagine letting go of any negative feelings, any discomfort, and then to aim her palms outward.

She listened as we continued to walk, her face still distorted in pain, and she told me she was a physician. Hello! Here I was telling a doctor that hands are healing! But get this: She finished the race and the next night at the awards dinner thanked me for helping her finish. She said she had never heard the suggestion that I had given her, and we talked about the importance and meaning of moving through difficult moments in life. How everything happens the way it is supposed to at the exact right moment.

At 8 P.M. I came into town. I was at mile eleven. Timothy was barely awake.

This course is a bit strange in that when you come into town, you can see the finish line, but then you turn to run up a hill out of town for a mile, turn around, and come back. So mile eleven also is mile thirteen. Miles eleven to thirteen felt like the longest two miles ever. I wondered how it would feel at mile twenty-four.

I retrieved my special-needs bag and got stuff to eat, grabbed my long-sleeved shirt, and headed back toward the crowd. By 8:30 P.M. I was back in town. I asked Bob, "Am I going to make it?" referring to the seventeen-hour cutoff. "Oh, definitely! I've done the math!" he reassured me.

It was getting dark and chilly. I came to the aid station near the bar where the volunteers were getting sillier and sillier each time I passed. "You go irongirlllll," they called out more slurred each time around. I danced with them on one stop. The music was incredibly loud.

At mile sixteen I put on my long-sleeved shirt, which had

been wrapped around my waist, and got more to eat and drink—a little salt, some chips, another GU, some Endurox R4, and off I went. It was pitch black. In between the generator lights I couldn't see anything. And then the fog began to roll in. I didn't have a glow stick and I was running alone and began to get a little spooked.

I saw a chair when I got to the aid station at mile eighteen. I asked if I could take a seat. Wow. It was one of those cheap lawn chairs, but I felt like I was on the most comfortable chair in the world. By this point I had been moving for more than fifteen hours. To sit for a moment was heavenly. I knew many would not agree with this approach, but it felt too good and after stretching a bit, I felt like a new woman.

Before I got too comfortable, a woman walked by wearing a TEAM-IN-TRAINING T-shirt. I was so happy to see another person that I quickly caught up to her. Jackie was from Kansas City, and there were nine members on her team. I told her about our team in California and how it inspired me.

We walked to mile nineteen and decided to pay attention to our time. We walked with a little bit of a jog and a lot of talking. I needed to pee about twice every mile. Jackie kept the pace and I would catch up and walk again.

At mile twenty I announced, "We are keeping a fifteen-minute-per-mile pace and if we keep it up we will definitely make it!" We were still walking, but trying to jog. I began feeling a wave of nausea and Jackie suggested drinking Coke. Ewww. I tried some Coke at the next aid station, just a couple of sips, and it helped.

Suddenly my cousin Michael appeared from the darkness. He tried to get me to go faster . . . as if! He ran about three paces ahead of us. I kept jogging, and Jackie did too. We made it to mile twenty-two. This was the farthest I had ever run in my life.

I had a little inner victory going as I kept moving forward.

Michael kept going and talking and talking. He was a great diversion, though Jackie pulled ahead of us, I think to get some quiet. Mile twenty-three was uphill. I ran that mile in thirteen minutes. I knew I could make it in before midnight. Plenty of time.

It was 11:30 P.M. when I saw mile twenty-four. Michael kissed me good-bye and passed the torch to Bob, who began to pace me for the end . . . that two-mile loop that leaves town and returns again.

Surprisingly, Bob was not his usual calm self. He was filled with nervous excitement and told me to keep jogging. "From now on, you can't walk at all," he said. Well, that didn't go over too well, so I walked. He was beside himself. I think if he could, he would have picked me up and run with me in his arms just to be sure I made the cutoff. But I knew I was going to make it and told him not to worry.

It was Bob's personal schedule I followed for the last twelve weeks of my training. It was Bob whom I came to with my training questions. It was Bob's willingness to reschedule his workouts so I could do my own . . . Bob's support, love and presence throughout the whole long year that saw me to the finish line. And during all this time he was training for Ironman Canada, which was two weeks later.

He was hopping up and down, running backward and forward just wanting me to move a little faster. I knew my pace, I knew the time, and I just kept moving forward. Perhaps I was a bit ignorant of the reality. In hindsight, I really could have missed the cutoff. I asked him to tell me a story.

"Once upon a time there was a girl who missed the cutoff of her first ironman by three seconds because she wouldn't move a little faster." This was so intense for Bob. He was trying to impart to me that I could DNF by seconds because I was taking my time. I had looked at the cutoff as a goal. Like a credit-card limit. That's what I had to spend—seventeen hours.

It was 11:43 P.M. when I reached mile twenty-five. I was feeling relaxed with lots of energy.

11:55 P.M. Mile twenty-six. Bob was still with me and things were getting pretty exciting.

11:56 P.M. Bob kissed me good-bye and leaped away like a gazelle. Later I heard how he jumped barricades, climbed six-foot walls, was caught in the arms of spectators and eventually the crowd stepped back to let him through. Bob told me, "It was like the parting of the Red Sea."

As I entered the arena, I held a picture of Emily and the emotion began to well up. I began to cry and could barely breathe. I made my way around the final turn before the chute. There were hundreds of people there . . . all cheering and screaming and high-fiving the whole way. The scene will be forever etched in my mind.

I looked up at the clock—16:57:25—and I thought to myself, "Hey look! I have plenty of time!"

There was Bob, all smiles, reaching out for me, a medal in his hand. Timothy was fast asleep in the Baby Jogger, face tipped up to the stars.

At 11:57:44 P.M. I came across the finish line with a big smile, arms up high, holding the picture of Emily. Bob picked me up into the air—just scooped me right up. "I did it! I am an iron-man!"

Just to be able to take on this challenge I thought was impossible and then to be able to do it makes me see myself in a way I've never seen myself before. But it's hard to explain. I have searched for a way to describe the indescribable. I feel as though I climbed this huge mountain, saw an incredible vista, and now

I am back on the ground, trying to relate what it looked like. I suppose there are words . . . somewhere . . . but it's like trying to describe childbirth or God or making love. It is so incredibly personal and intimate. The ironman was way more than I had ever expected: more enjoyable, more beautiful, more peaceful, more fun, more exciting, more spiritual, more emotional, more social. Just more.

Terry, Bob, and Timothy live in Alexandria, Virginia. Triathlon remains a focal point in their family.

SWIM TO VICTORY

LINDA COFFIN

DATE OF BIRTH: JUNE 4, 1941

RACE: HAWAII IRONMAN 2000

TIME: 16:36:16

I can do the distance. I know I can do the distance. I swam the distance in the pool, I swam it in the lake. I can't put into words or explain the fear I experience on the swim. It used to be that people would plow over me. But it moved beyond a fear of getting hit to simply being anxious in the water. My son Tim, who is a professional triathlete, said, "Mom, just stand on the beach until everyone leaves, then get in and swim."

I didn't stand on the beach as Tim suggested because I met Katy Knight-Perry, a sixty- to sixty-four-year-old age-grouper and some of her friends at the Masters Women's Breakfast two days before the race. "Oh no, you don't want to be standing on the beach," she said. "You get in with us and tread water, then start swimming when everyone else swims." I thought, 'If they can do it, so can I.' We treaded water and talked as if we were at a country-club social. Ann Marie DeMonte was sending out an invitation. "Now, Monday night I'm having a party and everybody is to come." Their comfort in the midst of fifteen hundred swimmers relaxed me. Ethel Autorino, who was seventy, provided some last-minute advice. "Don't worry about it. Everybody finds their own place." All these young guys were all around us and she wasn't worried.

When the race started I swam next to Ethel. I didn't hang on her. I didn't *need* her, but I saw her all the way out to the boat and it was wonderful. The only distraction I had was a cramp in my foot just before the end. I had to stretch it out and a man in a kayak came along to check on me. Finally it relaxed. I still had the best swim of my life. I swam the whole thing freestyle from the start. I've never done that. Never.

My first triathlon—Dave's Triathlon—was nineteen years ago. I'm a nurse practitioner in a small, rural family practice in Vermont and worked for a physician who organized a triathlon for friends and families in our area. I did it and my son, who was about ten at the time, started doing it too. There was no clock. Everyone brought food, and it was a big, summer family event. I had been running since I was thirty-four, and when I turned forty I bought a bike. Friends encouraged me to take the next step and enter a triathlon so I started swimming that summer, backstroke, because that's what I knew.

In 1981 I did the Burlington Triathlon. For several years I continued to do that event and Dave's Triathlon. Then about four years into it, I developed my swim phobia. At the Burlington Triathlon the water was so wavy I panicked and got onto a boat.

I was freaked and kept saying to myself, 'This is the best thing. I did the best thing. I did what I needed to do,' but I couldn't forget it that week. 'You trained the whole summer, and you got out of the water. You didn't even get out to the first buoy.' I kept beating myself up.

The next year I began having anxiety the week before the race. I was sitting in a conference, thinking about getting in the water that next week. I was hyperventilating right there in the room. I decided that I didn't need to put myself through that anymore. For the next four or five years, I went back to running as a triathlon relay-team member.

Then my son Tim wanted to qualify for Worlds. I went with him to qualifying races because he wasn't old enough to rent a car. I loved to go anyway and I began to see that some races had different swim waves of people at the start. They'd have age-groupers go in—say, all women over forty with men over sixty. Each time I'd go to a race, I'd think, 'I could do this again.'

The next summer, in 1993, I decided I was going to do triathlons again. I had taught myself to freestyle in 1982, but no matter how much training I did, I never got to use it in a race because I'd get so anxious and hyperventilate, and then flip over on my back. On my husband's suggestion, I went to a hypnotist. I still listen to her tape every day before a big event. The weekend after seeing the hypnotist, I went to Indiana with Tim to do the national qualifier and had a great swim. I didn't swim freestyle the whole way, but I had a pretty good swim.

Tim qualified for Worlds and I didn't, but I didn't care. I was happy to be there and was twelfth in my fifty to fifty-four age division. Two days after Tim qualified, I got a call from USA Triathlon: "Hey, Linda, would you like to go to England because two people aren't going and you're next in line?" I was thrilled. I did go and got tenth in my age division. I made it to Worlds again the next year and went to New Zealand in 1994. It was fun to be with these women my age who were interested in doing all this crazy stuff and still live full lives besides.

In 1997 Tim qualified for the Hawaii Ironman as a pro. It was his first time doing an ironman distance. As I watched I thought, 'I'd like to do that.' But I didn't tell anyone. I started swimming longer to see if I could do the distance. In 1999 I entered the lottery and didn't get picked. In 2000 I entered and when I came home after being out of town for a while, there was The Letter. "Oh my God." I had to decide to train or not, to commit or not. I had to do a half ironman race to get approval to compete in Hawaii, so I went to a half-ironman in Tupper Lake, New York. I felt great, but I had a rotten swim. I got through it—but I flubbed around in the water for twenty minutes longer than I needed to. So I went into the swim in Hawaii nervous I would have another repeat performance. I was elated when it was over and I actually swam freestyle the whole way.

The volunteers were wonderful in the change tent. I got my bike and started the ride and it was all I could do not to cry when I went past that crowd on Palani Road. *Oh my gosh, I'm here. I did that water. I did that swim.*

I went out on the bike and used mindfulness training I had practiced for years. I think our human tendency is to anticipate, 'Well, when I get off the bike, then I'll blah, blah, blah,' or 'I'll probably make it there at such and such a time, and then I'll run this or that.' I kept catching myself and saying: 'No, I'm by this NO PARKING sign right now on the Queen K, and the bougainvillea on the side of the road is stunning.' I was making myself be there by noticing the sensory things around me, bringing myself back to the present moment. To me the scenery—lava and all—was gorgeous, not boring. *Thank you, God, for these flowers. Thank you for the grass.* It was definitely a spiritual experience as well as a physical one.

Drink, eat your GU, hold on to that bike, watch the wind, and watch what you're doing instead of anticipating and getting away from the moment. It was so, so windy on the way to Hawi. It was that same gusting crosswind on the way back too.

I saw people that were knocked over by the wind. *How can I still be up?* But I stayed up. It was a very big relief to get to the transition area in one piece, and smiling.

Off the bike I felt good and ready to run and walk. Besides the cramping on the swim, I had cramping on the bike. I didn't want to force myself to run as long as I could or as much as I could and risk more cramping, so I walked and ran. I watched the time; all I wanted was to finish within the midnight hour.

When the sun started going down, I was midway through Alii. It was ethereal. I was happy to have the presence of mind to look around and appreciate where I was. It was lovely. The people were wonderful.

It was a relief to get to the Energy Lab and I started running again from there. It was about 9:30 P.M. but I didn't step anything up. I just did what I could do, and I felt that minute to minute, I didn't know if I could make it because anything could happen. The first marathon I did years ago, I got a cramp in my left leg and could not get it out. It was probably two-tenths of a mile away from the end or less, and I was on the ground. I knew that anything could happen. This was the first time I ever put my body through this lengthy exertion, and I really wanted to finish. When I rounded the corner on Alii though, I ran to the finish line.

I can't believe it. I can't believe I made it to this day. Those years ago thinking I would like to, and then I did. But I wasn't alone. It wasn't just me doing it. I really felt the presence of God with me—and my dad, who's dead, and my baby sister who died. I asked all my personal saints—my friends and relatives—to join me in a transcendent way with their strengths uniting with my efforts.

There was so much help from everyone. My husband, Jon, was a positive supporter. Instead of, "Oh, really? This again? Do you have to do that again?" he had said things like: "Whatever you need to do, do it." My whole family, too. I usually have the grandchildren stay overnight and they didn't that much during the summer I trained because I couldn't get up the next morning and train if a little one was there. And Tim—he wrote me a three-page plan that I looked at and used every day. I did everything he said. He didn't qualify that year so he wasn't able to race in Hawaii. I had to consider doing this alone when he didn't make it. But you do it alone anyway. You're out there alone; it's a solitary experience for everyone.

I don't know if I'll do another ironman. It's similar to being asked if I wanted to have another baby right after having my first one. It's too soon to know. After the Ironman (and after childbirth) I was both supremely elated and exhausted. Of course, I went on to have four more babies . . . but this time it seemed as if I had given birth to myself.

Linda Coffin, from Grand Isle, Vermont, is the mother of five and a grandmother of six.

DNF

Did not finish.

DATE WITH A LORRY

GORDON CHARLES ROSS
DATE OF BIRTH: DECEMBER 12, 1964
RACE: ABERFELDY TRIATHLON 1995
TIME: DNF

You must be bloody mad!" my mum said when I told her what I was going to do at the weekend. Good job she never found out what really happened.

About six o'clock in the morning there were about twenty of us "nutters" in Aberfeldy for the ironman-distance triathlon. I can't remember why I did it exactly. It was just something I wanted to do. I had done a lot of training but not, of course, enough.

The swim was at the Aberfeldy Community Centre, in a twenty-five-metre pool (not unusual in Scotland for obvious reasons), so we swam about 150 lengths, after which you come out dizzy. Fortunately the swim has since been moved to a loch, but it is *cold*. A neoprene cap is a must.

Being a reasonably good swimmer, I was first out of the pool. I made my transition in the community centre, which was practically empty—an eerie feeling. When I started the bike I was leading, but I knew it wouldn't last.

It didn't. I was soon caught by two strong cyclists and never saw them again. The cycle was one big circuit through the central Highlands of Scotland. Aberfeldy is a small country town. The ride is lonely; mostly you have sheep for company.

After about one third of the bike, I approached a roadworks with a traffic light. It was red—just my luck. There was a lorry coming straight toward me and not enough room for both of us. I decided to chance it. I cycled through the red light and into the roadworks, thinking I could come out the other end and the lorry could pass. Big mistake. Doing about 30K I suddenly saw an enormous hole in front of me. Too late to do anything but try to bunny-hop the hole. It nearly worked. Unfortunately my carbon Zipp back wheel hit the edge of the hole and shattered. I was catapulted over the handlebars. I crashed to the ground and lay unconscious for a couple of minutes. When I came to, there was a worker standing over me asking, believe it or not, if I wanted a drag on his cigarette. I would have laughed if I hadn't been in so much pain.

I was rushed to Stirling Hospital, but luckily nothing was broken. In the ambulance, the medics started to take my pulse. I told them they didn't need to because I had my heart-rate monitor on. "That's handy," one of them said, as I held out my wrist monitor that displayed my heart rate.

In the hospital I became infamous for filling up "pee receptacles." I had hydrated with about two litres of fluid just before the crash and was not burning it off. I couldn't stop peeing. I still wonder if I could have gotten in the *Guinness Book of World Records* for my "achievement" that day.

Half an ironman was no ironman as far as I was concerned. DNF, after all. The disaster in Scotland made me more, not less, determined to finish an ironman. I didn't tell my mum. I drove down to the Black Country in England and did the Longest Day Triathlon about two months later. I finished in 12:49, but collapsed at the end of it. For some reason my body hadn't absorbed the water and High Five I drank during the race and, soon after, I began vomiting. I didn't know where I was and wandered around like a drunkard, looking lost. Lucky for me someone noticed I looked 'weird,' and I was taken to the hospital for a second time. I was hooked up to a drip and spent the night there.

So one smashed carbon wheel, two hospital visits, and a lot of wasted time and money later, I could proudly say I had done my first one and a half ironmans. But please don't tell my mum.

Gordon Charles Ross, originally from London, is an English teacher at the University of Jena in Jena, Germany. He went on to compete in the Sachsenman in Moritzburg, Germany, in 1999, finishing in 11:11. He says entering Ironman Europe is in his future. His mum is on to him.

FALSE START

CHRIS LEGH

DATE OF BIRTH: NOVEMBER 18, 1972

RACE: HAWAII IRONMAN 1996

TIME: DNF

The day I embarked on that first ironman, I think I was in the best form ever. I lacked experience, but I was keen for a strong day.

Earlier that year I had come to America—to Boulder—to train for the World Long Course Championship. I was racing as a pro and was lucky enough to hook up with Mark Allen and Greg Welch. Many people who go to Boulder to train tire as they go throughout the season. Fortunately I seemed to get stronger. I was holding my form. Because of that, Mark and Greg thought I'd do well at the ironman distance. I couldn't resist—it's the pinnacle of the sport.

I went to Muncie, Indiana, to compete in Worlds and got eleventh. Then I went to the Half Vineman and won, earning my invitation to Kona.

After returning to Boulder I soaked up all the advice I could get from Mark and Greg. My run started getting longer, my bike rides extended by several hours. I didn't mind the extra distance. I can ride forever in Boulder—in the mountains—it's like playing, really. Ever since I was seventeen, when I entered my first triathlon, the Ironman definitely appealed to me. It was a mystery—three sports on a Hawaiian island. It's one of the toughest days in sport.

My swim was average at fifty-two minutes. I had work to do but I was amongst the top guys. On the bike I climbed that first hill and made the turn onto the highway. Dave Scott rode past me, but soon we were both stuck behind a pack that wouldn't move. In frustration Dave passed on the right side and I followed him. I knew it was illegal but the other fellows were blocking and it was impossible to get by. An official motored up beside me and slashed my number with a marker. "Why didn't you pull Dave Scott over?" I asked. The official shrugged, "I didn't see that," he said.

What a setback, and I wasn't even two miles into the bike course. I shook it off and got going again. Ahead, I rode up to another big group of riders—at least fifteen of them. This time, learning my lesson, I made sure to pass on the left. The now-familiar hum of the motorcycle approached and a draft marshal pulled me over, this time for taking too long to pass. The rule is fifteen seconds to pass a person. Well fifteen times fifteen—do the math—it's a long time. I didn't take that long. "You're out!" he said after giving me a second mark on my race number.

I didn't even get to the airport. This time I was less than ten miles into the bike ride. My race amounted to nothing more than a swim in the ocean. I stood there as racers whizzed by. I had done the training, I thought. 'I'm here, I might as well do the ride.' So I started on my way again until I saw a lonely, dejected figure on the side of the road. It was Sian Welch, Greg's wife. We had trained together all summer. She had been disqualified, too. I pulled over and we sat together commiserating. We decided we couldn't be bothered with the race anymore. We rode back to the hotel, cleaned up, and went back out on the course—this time as spectators.

That year officials really cracked down. But the rules are there for good reason and they're quite simple, actually. You ride in a straight line, ten metres apart. It has simplified racing. There were a few casualties that year, myself included, but all in all, racing in Ironman has improved because of it.

The following spring I raced the Aussie Ironman and qualified for Hawaii again. It was a strong field and I had a great day, running into third. But most rewarding was getting to the finish line.

Chris Legh is a professional triathlete from Donvale, Australia. He returned to Hawaii in 1997 and to the horror of spectators (and viewers of NBC's race coverage) collapsed yards from the finish. He underwent emergency surgery to remove a portion of his large intestine, which had died due to severe dehydration. But he more than recovered, placing second in three ironman races, along with a fifth-place and eighth-place finish in Hawaii the following two years. Chris won the inaugural Ironman California in 2000.

IRONMAN IS AN EVIL MISTRESS

BRUCE LYNN

DATE OF BIRTH: JUNE 4, 1947

RACE: IRONMAN FLORIDA 1999

TIME: DNF

Dadgum that chicken sandwich! It tasted delicious. It smelled good and looked good and looked cooked—with black stripes running across the white flesh. *Note to self: The next time you do ironman do not eat questionable food the night before the race.*

I woke up race morning feeling like someone was using my forehead for batting practice. It was like a bad omen. I took a couple of Advil, ate a banana, and went to the race site. I had been through this pre-race ritual at least thirty-six times before, but I still get nervous every time. And this was "The Big One."

I became a triathlete after watching the Hawaii Ironman on television. Now here I was about to attempt *the* distance. For months all I had thought about was this race. I visualized the swim, the bike, and the run over and over again. It became an obsession, really. I'm an assistant purchasing director for the Florida Highway Patrol. Even my mouse pad at work was an Ironman Live product. I bookmarked the Ironman Florida home page on my computer and clicked on the ever-growing list of participants each day. I'd scroll down to my name and stare at the letters. That was me, all right. I was entered. There was no backing out.

The sand on the beach felt cold under my feet. The air was damp and a breeze was blowing. When the swim started I got to the back of the pack and settled in to grind out the two-loop course in the Gulf of Mexico. Even though the crowd was pulling away from me, I fell into a rhythm, playing the usual mental games. I sang every song I knew in my head. I remember singing "Amazing Grace." Perhaps that was another bad omen. I tried to remember every race I had done and every teacher I had in school (Sister Anita, Sister Maria Goretti, Sister Rose Miriam . . .). Anything to pass the time.

The first lap was over and fifty minutes had gone by. I felt good because I knew if I kept the same pace I wouldn't get yanked from the course. My biggest fear was not making the two-hour-and-twenty minute swim cutoff. On the second lap the pack had really thinned out. I saw a guy breaststroking the whole 2.4 miles. Halfway through the second loop, I came to the realization that the officially sanctioned swim course and my swim course were not one and the same. I kept drifting to the west. After I overheard one of the kayakers say, "We didn't move the transition area to Pensacola," I started worrying about the cutoff. I couldn't bear looking at my watch for fear of missing it. Finally the race clock appeared: I was under two hours. I pulled up on land at 2:04 into the race. *Note to self: The next time you do this race understand that the Gulf of Mexico is a big place. Know where you are going.*

As I jogged up the ramp toward the changing tent, I heard a voice call my name. "Bruce, you made it!" yelled my training partner. It was great to see a familiar smiling face. We had talked about doing ironman together, but as a graduate student she couldn't make the time commitment. So I was doing the race for both of us. I changed and began the bike course with 1,544 people in front of me and 15 people and two motorcycle cops behind me. Things were going smoothly for about twenty miles and then the baseball bat came back. Only this time it hit me in the gut. I started redepositing the Gulf along the shoulder of the road.

I began to feel that, perhaps I wasn't supposed to be there. Had I not picked up my bike from the shop when I did, after its pre-race tune-up, I surely wouldn't have raced. I took it in on a Monday and planned to pick it up Wednesday. I was passing by the shop Tuesday after work and decided to pick it up early, if it was ready. It was and I took it home. The next morning the headline in the local section of the Tallahassee newspaper read, LOCAL BIKE SHOP BURNS TO GROUND. Apparently somebody decided to torch the place, and all the bikes in the shop were fried. Except mine. I took that as a good omen to do the race. But perhaps I had interfered with fate, and now I was paying the price in a different way.

I got off my bike and reenacted Bob Kempanien's marathon when he hurled orange Gatorade on national television. It was violent. After three spews I realized I was trading places with the last person in the race, and the two deputies on motorcycles confirmed this. The cops called for an ambulance and although they said I wasn't Code Three (I don't watch *ER* enough to know what that means), I knew I was extremely dehydrated and my race was over. *Note to self: The special-needs bag also is good for depositing the previous night's dinner once the stomach is finished processing it.*

I got a ride to the med tent and lay there drinking through my arm. Folks were walking by with pepperoni pizza. "Are you hungry?" asked a young girl. "Do you want something to eat?"

"Only if you don't mind me giving it right back to you."

I was able to take a shower and lie down, thanks to friends with a room at the race site, and managed to get up and see a few members of my triathlon club finish, although I made a couple of trips behind the dumpster.

I felt like I let myself down in a sense. I had never DNF'd before. Maybe I had obsessed about the race too much. It may have been stress. It may have been dehydration. I realized one of the worst things to do before a race is to stay out in the sun for two hours, walk around the expo, and not drink enough water.

But I had put in the time. Plus I had personal bests at St. Anthony's Triathlon and Gulf Coast Triathlon earlier that year. When I consider the time I trained for this race and how well my training partner and I got along, that made it worth it. We did so many rides together, so many runs together. It was really a good relationship. Triathlon is about camaraderie. You're with people you know, having a good time, experiencing the same things. To me, that's worth more than finishing.

Still, I felt like I had let something good get away. Like the girl that got away. And ironman is an evil mistress. I'll get her back.

Bruce went on to DNF in the next two triathlons he entered (the triathlon trifecta) but finished one after that, placing second in his age group. He plans to enter and finish an ironman soon.

THREE HUNDRED AND SIXTY SECONDS LATE

JANICE KING

DATE OF BIRTH: APRIL 24, 1968

RACE: IRONMAN USA 1999

TIME: DNF

The day began at 3 A.M. with scrambled eggs, toast and pasta. Another two hours of sleep before we were ready to face the day. My husband, Marshall, his sister Megan, and I headed into the quaint Adirondack town of Lake Placid to compete in Ironman USA.

My main fear during the swim was losing my goggles. A serious problem for most racers, but especially for me because I wear contacts. There were so many people—so many elbows, so many arms—I was sure I would get knocked in the head. I decided to stay away from the buoys (lines that were left out from canoe races earlier that week) and instead swim wide. That served me well until the second loop, when I went off course for a while. My hands were beginning to get numb by the end.

The strippers had me sit down before they got my wet suit past my butt, so we wrestled around a lot there. I got dressed. This time it was a wrestling match with my bike shorts over wet legs. Then I decided to use the bathroom, so I had to wrestle them down and up again.

It was cool—especially so after coming out of the chilly lake, riding in the wind, and catching air on the downhills. It was smart to wear my arm warmers—I needed them.

Coming in after the first loop I knew I was slower than planned. The volunteer held my special-needs bag for me as I rummaged through it. I wished she had dumped it on the ground so I could see all that was in there because I did not see and forgot I had pretzels and chips, which I would have liked later.

I ate three bars and started eating a fourth, but couldn't finish it. I washed them down with three Power Ades. Heading out to the second loop I felt bad. I knew it was 1:15 P.M. and I had only four hours and fifteen minutes to make it. The first loop had taken me four hours and twenty-five minutes.

I felt like I was going so slow. I had no energy. I was wondering, "Should I quit now? Is it possible for me to do a negative split?" I tried to stay positive. Another cyclist gave me encouragement. Actually he seemed to be there for me every time I was doubting myself.

I did not want to eat anything sweet. I stopped at an aid station to force myself to finish my Snickers bar—the only thing I ate on the second loop. Only when I started the out-and-back portion of the course did I feel better. I went to the washroom two or three times on the second loop—only once on the first.

After the out-and-back I knew I had just more than 20K to go. I thought I still could make it. Until that point I had my doubts. Until that point I was okay with not being an ironman that day. Then I realized how much I wanted it. If I had a chance, I had to push it. And I did. The last hour I went faster than I ever thought was possible for me. Where did that come from? Why did I not train harder? It must have been adrenaline. I pushed and pushed. I hyperventilated a few times.

Gained composure, pushed and pushed. I reached the big bastard hill at the end. Or so I thought. But no, that wasn't it. Finally the big bastard hill was before me. *I can do it.*

"Is the course still open?" I yelled to the volunteers at the turn into town. No answer. I was excited. I changed my Cateye to the time; it was ticking. I can't remember now if it had passed the key time. I wasn't really sure what the key time was, so I ignored it and kept pushing.

Oh no, runners on both sides of the street! No one cleared the way for me. Fuck!

"Bike on course! On your left! On your right!" *Oh forget it!* I went around. I weaved my way cussing and hyperventilating until finally I turned off. My brother ran with me. I asked him if I had time. He said he thought so. I knew he was lying but in case he wasn't, push, push, push. I battled hyperventilating and crying. Pedestrians on the street. "Move!" Finally the end. Volunteers told me to stop. I stopped. The timing mats were in front of me.

"Did I make it?" I asked.

"No," they said. I fought back tears.

"How much time?"

"About ten minutes." I bawled. I didn't get off my bike. I straddled the top tube and leaned over my handlebars and wept. Later I learned I missed the cutoff by an even narrower margin—six minutes.

A volunteer removed my timing chip. I started to walk with my bike, continuing to cry. A wonderful volunteer came up and put her arm around me and took my bike. She told me her husband never makes the bike cutoff. It made me feel better. She helped me put my bike away and I thanked her. I got my transition bag and walked out.

My dad, my brother, and his wife, Laurie, were waiting for

me. I got hugs from everyone before calling my mom at the pay phone. She told me Paula Newby-Fraser dropped out of the run. I was in good company.

Waiting for the elevator at the hotel, a group of teenagers asked me if I had done the ironman. I told them by how much I missed the bike.

"Did you do the whole 112 miles and the swim?" they asked.

I told them I had, and there was a chorus of "cools" and "wows." I had to fight so hard to keep from breaking down.

Before, during, and after my shower I cried. But I put on a happy face and went on to cheer Marshall and Megan. They did great. I was so happy for them. It made me all the more determined to try again. The next day I signed up for next year.

Looking back, the experience was truly a positive one, although it didn't seem that way at the time. First of all, it was so much fun to be part of such an amazing event. We were treated like professional athletes by the spectators at the parade and the volunteers who helped us during the race. Second, I had spent so much time training I felt like I belonged at the starting line. I met so many people through clinics and group rides and swims that I felt part of a community. I certainly had a lot of people to cheer for during the run. Third, a lesson in failure or not achieving one's goal was, in the end, also good for me. I have been so fortunate in my life that things have come fairly easy for me. This experience was new. I learned a lot about myself and what motivates me.

Janice, a chartered accountant in Oakville, Ontario, returned to Lake Placid in 2000 and became an ironman finisher.

FAST FINISH

First-timers discover their talent.

OUT OF DARKNESS

BRENT LORENZEN

DATE OF BIRTH: FEBRUARY 27, 1972

RACE: IRONMAN FLORIDA 2000

TIME: 9:16:30

I was one of the last people hanging out in the transition area when race officials made their final push to get everyone to the race start. I got to the beach and found myself in a mass of people moving every which way.

Everyone tried to move forward and the officials tried to move everyone back. In the midst of this back-and-forth, I felt pretty calm. I was a good swimmer and felt confident about starting up front. When the cannon went off, we ran into the ocean. The water was pretty warm—warm enough that the pros couldn't wear wet suits but still cool enough that we age-groupers could. Obviously there was a lot of thrashing the first quarter mile, but it wasn't as bad as I thought it was going to be.

I grew up swimming and swam all the way through college. I don't even know how I first became aware of triathlon, probably watching the Ironman on television. It always had been in the back of my mind that once my swimming career was over I'd try this triathlon thing. I graduated from college in 1994 with a degree in biology and anthropology, but wanted to coach so I went on to get a master's in exercise physiology. I never found the time to get too serious about triathlon. I'd run a little bit off and on and ride my bike every now and then, but never committed to a real training program and didn't feel like I should enter a race if I wasn't prepared for it. After moving to Southern California, I began coaching high school kids for a club team and found the time to train for my first race in the fall of 1997.

I knew I was drafting off a group near the front and tried to stay with them. We came out of the water after the first loop. I was right in the middle of a group of ten or twelve, and we all got right back in for the second loop. Soon after, someone brushed the top of my head with his hand and swiped my swim cap off. It freaked me out for a second, thinking I might be disqualified for not having it, but then I got real. I wasn't going to stop and put it back on, so I let it go.

The last half mile I lost my group and swam on my own. I didn't know how many people were ahead, but I still felt like I was probably in a pretty good spot. I came out of the water to a cheering crowd and ran to the transition area for a quick change. I was just getting on my bike when someone told me I was second in my age group. I thought, 'Okay, that's pretty good,' but didn't really know where I was overall. A couple of miles into it I passed one guy, but wasn't sure which age group he was in. After a few more miles I passed another guy. This guy was one of the pros. I settled in and at the same time waited for people to start going by me because I knew there were people in the race who could blow me away on the bike. It wasn't until about thirty miles into it that I got passed. Then I passed somebody, but he passed me again. I decided to let him set the pace and rode about ten meters behind him.

Turned out I was seventh out of the water. A few spotters along the course told me how far I was behind the leader as I went by. I didn't understand this at first—I didn't realize I was that far in front—it took me a few times to figure it out. Sixth place overall was what they were telling me.

Around mile seventy-five the guy I was pacing off started to slow down. I debated for a while, 'Should I keep riding behind him, or should I go by him?' I had to go on. I went by him and that moved me into fifth place.

Between miles eighty-five and one hundred was tough. The road got rough and we were going into a little bit of a headwind. People had told me to expect a bit of a crisis around the eighty-mile mark on the bike. I was ready for it when it hit. But before I knew it, I was coming back into town. I heard the announcer as I was going through the change tent, announcing who I was and that it was my first ironman and I was up with the pros—that got me going faster.

I didn't expect to do that well. I was confident I could qualify for Hawaii and place in the top ten in my age group, but where I was in the race at that point exceeded what I thought I could do, on the bike in particular. I set the goal to qualify, but no matter what, I just wanted to finish. I probably would have been disappointed if I hadn't qualified, but at the same time I felt like I had come a long way in the last year and a half just to be able to compete and enjoy the experience.

Enjoying anything had been nearly impossible for me the year before. In the summer of 1998 I took a coaching job in New Jersey. That was the end of triathlon for a while. By the middle of October I began sinking into a depression. I didn't realize it at the time, thinking I was unhappy with the move. I knew depression had been an issue in my family, but I never understood it and didn't think I would ever be subject to it.

I had all kinds of sleep trouble and didn't feel like doing anything. Nothing had meaning for me. I didn't get any enjoyment out of anything, not even coaching. There were plenty of days where it took everything I had to get out of bed and do my job. I would break down and start crying for no reason and felt like I was living in a fog. I lost my ability to think rationally, and felt like I lost control of certain aspects of my life. I suffered an incredible sadness.

By October I wasn't training at all. It was so hard to feel like doing anything. I'd talk on the phone to my mom and she'd say, "You have to go out and do something. Just go for a walk," and it took every ounce I had to walk for half an hour. I couldn't fathom trying to run.

Then a couple of people at the school where I worked said, "You know, I think you need to talk to someone." Part of me thought the move had caused my depression, so if I left, I'd take care of it. That wasn't the answer, but that's how I looked at it at the time. I began seeing a psychiatrist and was on medication for a while, which helped pull me out of it enough to think more rationally and move through some decisions, although it was still definitely a roller coaster for a while.

In February 1999 I moved back to Southern California. During the next couple of months I continued to experience ups and downs, but was able to reflect on them more rationally. I could at least identify some of the contributing factors and ways to keep it under control.

One thing I've realized is that there were probably times in the past when I was right on the edge and, for whatever reason, I didn't fall into that depression. Growing up swimming was good for me in that exercise helped keep it from happening. I know there's more to it than that, but I think exercise does help me control it. I've also learned to identify when it starts coming on and talk myself through the feelings, look at them reasonably, and not make such a big deal out of this or that.

I also signed up for Ironman Florida. I made a commitment to finish an ironman and mapped out a training plan. I raced about once a month leading up to it. Now I'm definitely hooked.

I was even more hooked during my ironman, realizing how well I was doing. I got on the run ahead of the guy who I'd come in with. The first few miles of the run my stomach didn't feel very good and my legs hurt a lot. Going in I thought I could run a 3:30 marathon and if everything was going great, I could go 3:20. But I had never run a marathon before.

I'd planned on doing one back in February, but got hurt training for it. So yeah, I *thought* I'd like to run 3:30, but knew I could just as easily do 5:30. I checked my watch the first couple of miles and was running between a 7:00- and 7:30-per-mile pace. About four miles into it, three guys blew by me, one right after the other. I couldn't even think about trying to stay with them. One of them was in my age group; the other two were pros. I was still thinking to myself, 'Wow, I'm in the top ten right now, not too shabby—hang in there.' Yeah, it's a race, but more than anything it's a race with yourself.

Perhaps that's not so easy for pros to think when they have more riding on it. Hopefully I'll find myself in that situation at some point, but at that moment, I felt on track to reach the highest goal I set for the race. It was easy to feel good about what I was doing and concentrate on my own race. Although I was definitely keeping an eye out. It was a two-loop, out-and-back run course, so I had plenty of opportunities to see people. I couldn't help counting when the guys ahead of me started coming back the other way, and once I made the turn seeing how close people were to me and so on. For the most part I thought everybody looked fresh. I didn't think I was going to be able to run anybody down, but apparently a couple of guys ahead of me had total meltdowns and dropped out.

The second lap was a little more confusing because people were all over the place, most on their first lap. Between miles sixteen and twenty-one were toughest for me. I started to think about walking, but talked myself out of it. Near mile twenty I started drinking Coke at the aid stations and within a couple of miles I got revived. Of course knowing I had only five miles left helped too.

I came over a small hill and made a sharp turn into the finish line. I had visualized what it would be like to finish the way I wanted to and knowing I had exceeded those goals was over-whelming. My run split was 3:29—right on what I expected—and my overall time was 9:16.

I was incredibly happy, but there was more relief than I'd thought there would be and I was more mentally drained than I thought I would be. I wasn't sure exactly where I had finished, but pretty convinced I had gotten my slot to Hawaii. I ended up twelfth overall and second in my age group.

I've always been a big fan of endurance sports. Growing up swimming I value hard work and endurance and ironman struck a chord with me. Being able to qualify for the Hawaii Ironman means I'll be able to subject myself to the ultimate test. Given everything I experienced in terms of going through depression and being out of shape physically and mentally, it was very rewarding to be able to bounce back with such a high achievement. I don't think I could appreciate the high point of qualifying as much as I do without having come from such a low point.

Brent hopes to compete professionally some day. Whether or not he can race at the top, he plans to enjoy racing, training, and the experiences of meeting new people and seeing new places through triathlon.

THE LONG AND SHORT OF IT

JOANNA ZEIGER
DATE OF BIRTH: MAY 4, 1970
RACE: HAWAII IRONMAN 1996
TIME: 10:27:15

photo by robert oliver

It was still dark when I arrived at Kailua Pier, but the transition area was aglow with bright lights. As I walked through the crowds to get numbered and drop off my special-needs bags, everyone I bumped into seemed so somber. I felt like we were going off to war. I tried not to let that affect me, but the atmosphere seemed especially gloomy because nobody was very chatty. I hardly knew anybody, including which triathletes to be in awe of. I was naive about the triathlon scene, about racing, nutrition, equipment—you name it.

I got into the water pretty early to warm up and get a good spot close to the front. Paddlers hovered near the start line, keeping swimmers from inching too far forward. I was treading water—bobbing elbow to elbow with nervous triathletes—in cramped quarters as the bay filled up with hard bodies.

I struck up a conversation with the person next to me, also treading water. I don't even remember what we talked about, but when I ducked my head underneath to adjust my cap and goggles, I saw he had no legs. That put everything in perspective for me, immediately. I was completely impressed and amazed and it was the encouragement I needed right before the start, knowing he was going to do it too. Within a few minutes the gun went off and I started my swim.

Open water didn't intimidate me much. I had been on the swim team at Brown University, and having grown up in San Diego, I was a regular at the La Jolla Rough Water Swim from the time I was seven. I was more worried about the fifteen hundred people beating me up than the ocean swim itself. I'd seen it on television and it looked like mayhem. That's exactly what it was.

No matter what approach you take in the swim, no matter where you put yourself in the beginning, you get pummeled. Eventually I managed to get away from the masses and find open water. I could see a big group in front of me and worked hard to catch them and finally tail-ended them as I was coming out of the water. I was third woman, behind Wendy Ingraham and Ute Mueckel.

The transition area was a frenzy. I put on my jersey, got slathered with sunscreen, got on my bike, and proceeded to get passed and passed and passed. It didn't take long before people were riding by me in droves. With so many people around I didn't know where to ride; I worried about getting some kind of drafting or blocking penalty. People were yelling, "On your left, on your left—get out of the way!" I held my line as best I could and kept pedaling.

I had no preconceived notions of what kind of pace to hold. Whatever felt comfortable was what I did. As long as I felt comfortable, my pace was fine, I figured. I was clueless really, and at some point in the middle of the Queen K wished I had talked to more people or read more books—wished I had done my homework.

Unlike most first-time athletes, I didn't drive to Hawi or preview the Energy Lab. I had no interest in exploring the geography, thank God, because had I known what was coming—the monotony of the lava fields, the heat, and the wind—my pre-race anxiety would have been unbearable.

When I got to Hawi, volunteers handed me my special-needs bag packed with a peanut butter and jelly sandwich, cookies from the carbo dinner, a banana, and a bottle of sports drink. I had planned to have a picnic lunch out there, but I promptly tossed the bag in the bushes—there was no way I could eat. Even though I had consumed the same food during training, it was completely repulsive to me during the race. Knowing I needed something, I put a bar in my mouth but couldn't chew. I held it on my tongue hoping it would dissolve to a consistency that would allow me to swallow it.

I resorted to GU, which volunteers provided on the course, and drinking Coke. The sugar went right to my bloodstream and before I knew it I had a massive sugar buzz, which turned into a really bad cycle of up and down with sugar and caffeine. The more I took, the more I needed it. It was like drugs. I'd drink the Coca-Cola and instantly feel better so when I went by aid stations that didn't have it, I'd want to cry. There was truly a sense of panic: I was a cola junkie and that provided the only calories my stomach would allow.

I wondered if the pressing wind would ever stop. I saw a guy in front of me and noticed he was hurting too—really working hard—and I could tell he felt the wind as much as I did. That was a comfort. When I do ironman now, what helps me get through it is looking around and seeing how other people are doing to remind myself that I'm not the only one feeling the pain.

I was so excited when I saw the first airplane. The airport was a herald of the beginning of the end because it meant I was getting close to town. But once I got to the airport, I had this sudden realization that I would have to run a marathon, and that was a mental setback. I hadn't thought about running a marathon the entire time I was on the bike and suddenly I began to wonder what on earth I had gotten myself into.

See, I have a history of going into races grossly underprepared. I felt that way in my first ironman as much as I did my first triathlon in 1993, when I borrowed a bike from my swim coach's sister-in-law and without much running or biking signed up anyway. I swam well and then got passed by tons of people on the bike. Having to run after getting off the bike was more difficult than I had anticipated. I had no idea what I was getting myself into then either.

I also worried because I knew what a marathon felt like. I ran my first marathon in 1993 after moving to Chicago for graduate school. I was out one day, pokily running along the lakefront, when a guy ran up beside me and asked if I was running the Chicago Marathon. I didn't even know there was a marathon in town and having only run six miles at a time, explained that I wasn't that kind of runner. But it got me thinking and I ended up running nine miles that day. Well, actually eight miles, because I had to walk the last mile (read: crawled home). I was sore the next day but two days later I went out and did nine miles again, and felt fine. I figured I was as good as ready to do that marathon, and after a quick buildup to thirteen miles, toed the line at the start. I finished it in 3:32, but that last 10K really hurt. Although I was definitely more trained for my marathon in Hawaii, I knew I would start the run on fatigued legs and a huge energy deficit.

I put the dread of running a marathon out of my mind as soon as I reached Alii Drive. The crowds were cheering and once again I felt part of something. Their enthusiasm was infectious and I felt back in the game—ready to tackle what was next on my agenda.

I got to the transition area after almost six hours of riding and handed my bike to a volunteer, dropped my waist belt, quenched my thirst, went to the bathroom, got more sunscreen, put on a hat, and left the transition. It was quite a shockeroo to run that first hill out of the transition area.

I started having serious problems at mile six or seven. All that Coca-Cola, all that sugar, and all that caffeine—my bowels were rumbling. The first attack hit at mile six, where, fortunately, there was a Porta-Potti. As the bouts of diarrhea became more frequent it seemed there were fewer and fewer Porta-Pottis—not enough for my needs anyway. After a while I looked for a branch, a leaf, anything to get behind. I went behind a twig thinking, "Oh, okay, I'm covered, no one can see me." Of course, after three or four stops, I didn't care anymore.

To add to my misery it was hot—very muggy and hot. But the aid stations were just unbelievable: They had sponges, they had ice, they had water, cola, and sports drink. There was so much available and the volunteers were so helpful; they were such a comfort each time I arrived.

Except for stopping to go to the bathroom, I ran the first thirteen miles, even through the aid stations. After that I had to walk the aid stations. I didn't mind walking at all; in fact, it gave me something to look forward to, a treat every few miles.

Another treat was getting to watch the Natascha Badmann/ Paula Newby-Fraser duel. When I reached the Queen K Highway, the two of them were stride for stride coming back from the Energy Lab. I stopped and watched them go by. It was cool to see so close up. I was grateful, too, it wasn't me running that hard because I couldn't imagine having somebody right on my shoulder—especially for a distance like ironman. At that stage for me, racing the ironman seemed like an oxymoron.

And thus, I had no expectations for my finish. As I approached the turnaround in the Energy Lab, I watched people coming back, watched them push the limits of their mind and body—it gave me chills.

With it being such a long, lonely day, there was solace having so many people around. I didn't have the energy to talk, but I could sense the camaraderie. We all were going through every single emotion—from nervousness to elation: We were hurting, we felt good, we were in despair, we felt joy. All compacted into one day.

Coming into town for the last time and seeing crowds again, I knew the end was near. From Alii Drive to the finish—it's an eternity. I wanted so badly to be done, but still had a mile to go. That finish line was like the scene in the movie *Poltergeist*—you know, when the door just keeps getting farther away?

I always knew I would finish. Even though my stomach hurt, even though I wasn't feeling that great, even though I was walking the aid stations, there was no doubt. But when I finished, I just bawled my eyes out, I was so happy. I finished faster than I expected and was sixth in my age group and the tenth amateur.

Finishing so well made me realize that ironman was something I could do and, even though I had my troubles out there, I knew I would come back and do it again, and do it better. Crossing the finish line opened up a whole new door for me athletically.

I felt the same way when I made the Olympic Triathlon Team. I knew my skills were there and my fitness level was there, but I also knew what could happen in a race. There are a million factors out of your control and so much can go wrong. Especially in the draft-legal, short-course races, every second counts. If you have a bad transition, that could be it for you.

The starts are brutal. People jockey for position and it's just no-holds-barred. It's war. With ironman if you don't have a good swim, it's okay. Taking your time in the transition area is fine. You can go through projectile vomiting for forty miles and yet still come through it and have a good race. Not one part of the race counts so much that it can jeopardize your goal—and that's why I like it.

When pro triathlete Joanna Zeiger competed in her first ironman she was still an amateur, living and training in Baltimore, Maryland, where she had moved to begin her Ph.D. in genetic epidemiology at Johns Hopkins University. Joanna competed in the first-ever Olympic Triathlon race at the 2000 Sydney Games. One month later she finished her fifth ironman. Joanna was the only ironman finisher on the eight-member 2000 Olympic Triathlon Team.

WEIGHING IN AT IRONMAN

KATJA MAYER

DATE OF BIRTH: JANUARY 4, 1968

RACE: IRONMAN EUROPE 1992

TIME: 10:21:55

I always had problems with my weight as a child and young adult. There was always one diet after the other, but I never got rid of it. Even the sports I played in school didn't help. Neither did partying, but that's what I was doing as a typical eighteen-year-old. When I was twenty-one, a friend took me to watch a short-distance triathlon in a little town next to where I live. As I watched this race, I was amazed how happy people were when they finished. I wanted to find out for myself what created that happiness.

Of course, I couldn't run a 5K. Swimming wasn't a problem and I could ride my bike for 20K, but anybody can ride a bike for 20K; it's just a matter of pacing. But to run 5K? That had me worried, so I started running two minutes, walking one minute, and increasing that until I was able to run the distance. In 1990 I finished a very short triathlon without having to walk. I was pretty slow, but I was happy.

Happiness begets happiness and training begets more training. The next year, in 1991, I ran a marathon. I thought if I could run a marathon, then I probably would be able to do an ironman.

The year I trained for my first ironman I was studying mathematics and physical education at Munich University, I was working, and I was training—it was very hectic. Interestingly enough, my weight came down. Funny how running marathons and training for ironman will take care of that sort of problem. My weight has never been an issue for me since.

Race morning I was nervous and worried because there were so many unknowns. I had talked to many people and they all told me it's a hard day and to be patient. Could I finish? Would I go too hard, or not hard enough? What about the nutrition? Would I eat the right things to get me through the day? I had never done this before, and I was concerned. Plus I had all these people with me—my parents, my boyfriend and other friends— they were there to see me finish. It was great to have their support, but it was pressure, too.

Before the race started I went to check out my bike in the transition area. At other races I had seen people stick unwrapped Power Bars on the top tube of their bike, so I did that too. But being a novice and not knowing any better, I did it the night before, not the morning of the race. It had rained the whole night and my Power Bars had melted all over the frame. Mosquitoes and flies were stuck in it. I had to peel the mess off and go in search of alternate food sources—fortunately I found people who had Power Bars to spare.

The swim was a wave start because we swam halfway up a canal to a turnaround and swam back. There were so many people in such tight quarters, the water was churning. Amid the high waves though, I could see a huge banner that said, KATJA, GO! My family was walking along the canal with this banner. It was a nice surprise.

A not-so-nice surprise was that I got seasick in the swim. It was so bad I had to stop and throw up. I felt horrible and didn't know why. I just assumed I had gotten off to a bad start—I didn't attribute it to seasickness. But as soon as I got out of the water and stood on my feet, it was gone. I finished the swim in about 1:04.

My fans were waiting at my bike. It's a long transition area, and they were standing behind the fence. I yelled to them, "I just threw up on the swim!" My mom, of course, was concerned—she probably thought I should have stopped right then and there.

It poured rain all day. It was a terrible day, especially for spectators. But for me, the bike ride was perfect. There was nothing bothering me. I didn't care about the conditions because I couldn't change them. Everyone had to deal with them. I still feel that way when I race. In Hawaii it's the wind. So you have to ride in the wind—it's windy for everybody.

I picked a great race for my first ironman, though. I think going to Roth is the best first-time race because there are so many spectators and you're never on your own. There's something like a hundred thousand spectators around the course, and they are wild about the athletes. It's amazing.

I wrote down a timetable of when I thought I would be at specific points for my parents and my boyfriend. I had a range between this and that time to finish my swim, and then the bike between this and that time, and I was just way ahead of my predictions. My parents were waiting for me after the second bike loop and I didn't show up because I had already passed. My mother was really concerned. She heard an ambulance go by and was positive I was in it.

I felt great, but I still was somewhat anxious because I didn't know how I would feel on the run. But on the bike, I cruised. I didn't ever feel tired—not even on the hills. There was one hill—it's a famous hill in that race, called Solarer Berg—there were about twenty thousand people along the road cheering. It's probably 1K uphill, and it's like riding in the Tour de France. There's a very tiny aisle to ride up, but having all those people cheering at me, I flew up that hill—I didn't feel the hill at all. I got goose bumps there.

It's a three-loop bike course, so I got to experience that three times—50K, 100K, and 150K. I'm sure that's what helped me that day—my bike split was at 5:30.

My family and friends were waiting for me in the transition. I think the day was as much fun for my parents as it was for me. My parents were not at all interested in sports before I started doing triathlons. At home the word sport didn't exist, and here they were cheering me on in the pouring rain. They were so excited to be a part of the race.

I started the run and was able to maintain the same pace the whole marathon, again without any problems. My stomach was okay, my legs were okay, and it was just so much fun with all the spectators. It was nice that my boyfriend and my parents didn't stay together, so every three or four kilometers one of them was there to cheer for me. It made it easier because I knew just 2K down the road I'd see them again.

Even though I came into the race just wanting to finish it, I knew I would do that and started to think about my time. I knew I was doing well—much better than I could have anticipated—and thought if I could finish feeling the way I had felt all day, my time was going to be around eleven hours. As the marathon went on, I did some more calculating and realized, 'Wow, if I keep up this pace, I'm going to finish in ten and a half or even faster.' And that's what happened.

I began to cry the last five hundred meters. The end was so

overwhelming—the feelings that have been numbed by training and racing catch up to you. Ironman is such an effort, not only that day, but also the months before—all the training and the studies and holding down a job. It's a big effort, and one where only two years before I thought, 'Wow, ironman. That's something. I wonder if I could do it.' And then there I was, finishing an ironman.

I placed second in my age group that day and qualified for Hawaii—something I had never considered being able to do. I wasn't interested in my placing or anything. I wanted to finish and enjoy myself. I knew one day I wanted to race in Hawaii, but I didn't expect it to happen in the same year. Then I went to Hawaii and won my age group.

That's when I knew. After that finish I thought, 'That's it. I've found what I'm supposed to do.' I think everyone has something, but a lot of people don't ever find it or they don't even look for it. I'm so grateful to have found my passion.

Katja finished her studies and graduated in 1995. She opted then to turn pro instead of taking a university teaching job. She has raced in Hawaii every year since except in 1999, when as she explains, "The whole year was bad luck." She sustained injuries from bike crashes in two consecutive races that resulted in hospital stays, preventing her from qualifying for Hawaii. Instead she went to the inaugural Ironman Florida 1999—which she would have never done otherwise— and won. Good things can always come from bad situations.

PARTY ON!

TROY JACOBSON

DATE OF BIRTH: JUNE 16, 1969

RACE: LAKE SUNAPEE ENDURANCE
TRIATHLON 1990

TIME: 9:44:16

I was a sophomore at Westchester University in Pennsylvania. Wednesday before ironman my friends and I had a big party. We were just doing what you do in college—drink too much and stay out really late. Early the next morning my coach and I started the drive to Lake Sunapee, New Hampshire. I was pretty hungover—unbelievably hungover—and just getting sick all the way up. So was my coach, for that matter. He had been at the party, too. It was not a fun trip, and not ideal for the days leading up to an ironman race.

Race morning was pretty chilly—probably below sixty degrees. I didn't get a lot of sleep the night before, obviously nerves. Fortunately my hangover had worn off by then. I got up very early—around three hours before the race, at 4 A.M.—because I always read you have to make sure your body is ready to go. I was totally novice. I didn't like to eat a lot of food the morning of races so I just had a Power Bar. My bike was in good shape—that was all ready.

Ever since I got into triathlon back in 1988, I thought iron-

man would be a neat thing to do. I thought it would be the ultimate challenge. After doing a couple of half-ironman races and
several Olympic-distance races, I decided I wanted to try it.
That course was about an eight-hour drive so it made sense to
go there as opposed to going cross country. In fact, back then I
think there was the Great Floridian. That might have been it in
all of North America. There weren't all the ironman races there
are now, so Sunapee was a good choice. And it's beautiful there.
It's quiet, serene, a friendly town and the locals were really nice.

My parents came from Baltimore to watch. We stayed at a
lodge on a lake. There were about four hundred people in the
race, and there was a lot of hype about it. Back then ironman
was unique. Not everybody did them. Nowadays a lot of people
have done ironman so it's not a huge deal anymore, but back
then it was really a big thing. We previewed the course, and it
was brutally hilly. It was a five-loop bike and a three-time out-
and-back run, and it was very tough.

I thought I was well trained, but you never know. I had done
some one-hundred-mile bike rides. I hadn't done a marathon
yet, so I wasn't really sure about that. My goal was to finish, but
I also wanted to do well—place in my age group.

The water was crystal clear. I got in and went through this
process of swimming 2.4 miles. I didn't come from a swimming
background, so I had no idea what was going to happen. I
remember at one of the turnaround buoys, the leaders were
coming back and I still had a couple hundred yards to go, and I
thought, 'Oh my gosh, these guys are so fast.' My parents were
there when I got out of the water and told me I was fifteen minutes back. I thought, 'Jeez, it's going to be a long day.'

I ran to my bike and for some reason I instinctively touched
the back tire. It was flat. I couldn't believe it. My disc wheel was
flat. It was the worst luck. I yelled to my coach and he ran to his

car and got a wheel. The officials allowed for this. Instead of changing it, they allowed me to put on another wheel, but the wheel wasn't really set up for my bike. It was my training wheel and a bigger tire and not the fancy disc wheel I had. But I popped that on, figuring I lost another five minutes. Now I was twenty minutes behind.

It was cold. Especially when getting out of water and riding in fifty- to sixty-degree weather. At least it was sunny. I started to pass people right away. I wore one of those teardrop helmets from years ago. I had an Eddie Merck's steel bike with PSX tubing. It was a classic frame, but not exactly a triathlon bike.

I was drinking at every aid station, eating my Power Bars and trying to take in enough calories and fluids. Still, I had that unknown feeling of, 'Okay, what's it going to feel like on the fifth lap of this hilly bike course?' Every time the participants came back through town, we saw all the spectators there clapping for us. As I went around, my dad and my coach would yell, "You're X number of minutes behind and you're number whatever."

By lap three I was in third place. I was making up time. I was just five minutes behind. On lap four I was in the lead; it was an incredible feeling. I'd won a race earlier that year so I knew what it was like to lead. It motivated me more. But my lap splits became significantly slower. I think everybody's were; everyone was getting tired.

There was a thousand dollars for first place. That's a boatload of money for a college kid. That was definitely in the back of my mind. I came off the bike in first place, but only two minutes up. I put on my shoes thinking, 'How am I going to be able to run?' I'd never run that far after riding 112 miles on a hilly course. I had finished the bike in about 5:10.

My legs felt okay at the beginning. It was out and back three times, and again lots of hills. People were cheering and the lead vehicle was up there in front of me. It was cool, but I knew these guys were behind me trying to chase me down. A couple of them were the local New England studs who had done Hawaii Ironman before. Back then it was like, 'Oh my God. That guy has done Ironman. He's so awesome.' There was a pro woman there, too. She was with Team Pioneer, which was Pioneer Stereos. They sponsored a big pro team back then.

The run was somewhat shaded. Conditions were perfect: seventy degrees, no humidity, a light breeze. There was a bar at one point on the course and all these guys were out on the deck drinking and cheering for us. Every time I ran by, they'd yell my number and say, "You're in first place."

A top pro back then, who used to race on the Bud Light circuit years ago, was out on the course on a bike. He came up to me on the run and said, "Man, you're looking great." That really pumped me up.

On the second lap I actually started putting time on people, but I was feeling horrible. I started to fall apart. I think I ran the whole thing, but I felt bad, and my legs were sore. I just had that deep-down 'this really sucks' feeling. It's always tough. It doesn't matter who you are or how often you do ironman. But I didn't want to let that lead get away. I didn't want to sprint in an ironman.

The last part of the run was up the ski slope to finish at the lodge. I ran up that big hill—shuffled up that big hill—thinking, 'I can't believe this. I'm in first place—I might just win this thing.' And I did. I ran my first marathon in about 3:18. I crossed the finish line first. The second-place guy ended up about seven minutes back.

When I finished I wondered if there were any other races around that year because I felt so awesome, I wanted more of that feeling. There weren't and I didn't end up taking the qualifying spot—I waited until the next year. But I thought, 'Wow, if I could do this well in my first ironman, what could I do next time around?' I was interviewed by some magazine up in New England. At twenty years old, I was the youngest person ever to win an ironman-distance race. Of course, there weren't a lot of ironman-distance races around then, but that was kind of cool.

My parents thought I was crazy. That's what parents are going to think of you when you're riding your bike all day, and running and swimming. But like any parent, they're glad to see their son doing something he likes to do, and it was nice to pick up a grand too. It paid for the trip and put a few dollars in my pocket. I probably went home and spent it on a keg.

Troy Jacobson, a former high school football player, was looking for his athletic niche in college when he discovered triathlon. Now he is a pro triathlete and coach living in Baltimore, Maryland.

THE AURA OF ALII

TODD MURRAY

DATE OF BIRTH: MAY 25, 1963

RACE: HAWAII IRONMAN 1992

TIME: 10:07:40

At Mike and Rob's Triathlon in 1992 I placed fifth in my age group, which offered two qualifying slots for the Hawaii Ironman. The disappointment of coming so close and thinking I wouldn't qualify was hard to swallow. I listened intently at the awards ceremony, not completely hopeless. Finally they got to my age group. My heart fluttered when race officials announced that the winner wasn't eligible because of his pro status. Second place, same thing, also a pro. My palms were warm and I slid them against my shaven legs in hopes of drying them out. I had been a triathlete since 1984, but never considered doing an ironman. I didn't have the desire to go that long and even so, I didn't think I could finish. But something happened in 1992 and I thought, 'You know, maybe I could. Maybe I could finish one of those.'

I waited, suspended in limbo between the haves and the have-nots: those who have qualified for Hawaii and those who have not. The next guy, third place, accepted his spot. "Oh man," I kept repeating under my breath. Then fourth place took the final spot and I was left one away, wondering if I'd ever get this close again.

As I settled in to accept my fate, the announcer said, "And because we don't have anybody in this old age group, we're going to drop this slot into the men's thirty- to thirty-four age group." All of a sudden, Lisa, my wife now, but girlfriend at the time, screamed. Goose bumps ran down my body. They called my name and I gladly accepted my invitation to Hawaii.

I had entered Ironman Canada, which was two weeks later, but decided to drop out considering my good fortune. I wanted to save everything I had for Hawaii.

In addition I was trying to save everything I had for an engagement ring for Lisa. I thought Hawaii would be the perfect locale to pop the question. It's romantic, we'd never been there before, we had dated for four years, and I was ready to propose. In the end I just didn't have enough money. I was excited to go to Hawaii, but even if I finished I couldn't do what I really wanted to do there. I wanted my proposal to be part of our ironman experience.

So finishing became my singular focus. My main goal was to have fun and smile a lot. I visualized the perfect race over and over, but decided whatever problems I faced, I'd deal with them. I had seen too many people lose it and make matters worse. One of my favorite stories is about John Howard. He had a race in Hawaii when his derailleur fell apart on the bike ride. In the middle of nowhere, without tools, he believed it was over. Then he thought, 'Well, shoot, maybe I'll look for the part.' So he started back, found all his parts, found a bottle top to use as a screwdriver, and finished the race. I think that's a great attitude to have. No matter what, try to finish. I've only had one DNF and it still haunts me. I hate DNFs. I'm afraid of DNFing because I have a feeling it will be easier the next time.

Race morning I got in the water to warm up. I eyed everyone closely, noting who was who and the enormously high fitness level of everyone around me. Doubts about my training crept into my mind. I was intimidated by all the fit bodies. But I shook it off. I couldn't let myself do that—especially not minutes before the start. I have to have confidence that I've done the right stuff. It's too late to change. Lisa and my parents were watching from the seawall a short distance from the start. I swam over and said hi to them.

The race started and the swim was nothing like the horror stories I had heard about—no kicking, no hitting, definitely a bit crowded, but everyone seemed to find their pace. I had an hour to think about the rest of the day, without knowing exactly how long my day would be. While I could, I tried to let my mind go blank.

As soon as I got out of the water my mind was speeding. I didn't want to forget anything. I didn't want to forget the rules. Don't get in trouble here. Don't be too slow here either.

I got ready, jumped on my bike, and blasted up Pay and Save Hill with my heart-rate monitor beeping at me. There were so many people lining the street yelling that I got sucked into their energy. Sucked in until I reached the top and made myself think about the next 111 miles.

Out in the lava—out on the desolate Queen K—it's easy to listen to your breathing, watch your heart rate, and eat and drink when you need to. Out there you can concentrate. Sometimes too much. I cruised along for eighty miles and then it started to get hard. My concentration turned to the wind blowing in my face, my aching back, the people who were starting to pass me. I didn't like that.

The hills out on the highway in the wind were deceiving. I found myself downshifting, even when it didn't look like that big of a hill, but boy oh boy, I kept looking for easier gears.

Getting to Hawi was a psychological boost—the turnaround. I slowed down for my special-needs bag, but it wasn't there, and I wasn't going to stop. It was one of those things that didn't go as planned. So what? Keep going. This is not going to ruin your day.

The aid stations were great. They had everything I needed. I picked up a banana and some cookies and got back on track. I was fine. Until I reached the airport. I fell behind on my pace. I was alone, except for the wind. Everywhere around me was barren. I imagined the crowds back in town carrying me down Alii Drive to the transition.

I had never run a marathon and was anxious about running one now. I didn't know what to expect. The start of the run was a slap in the face. There's a huge hill out of the transition—that I walked up—then down into the pit and back up the hill. It was almost impossible not to go anaerobic, yet the crowds are there and I got caught up in the emotion. 'Yeah! Oh yeah! I'm doing Ironman!' That lasted until the lava. But until then Alii Drive was a comfort—all the people, all the green—it was a magic carpet ride to the Queen K Highway.

The Energy Lab was unpleasant, but not so much that I wanted to quit. I was hoping to run a 3:40 or better, but then again, never going that distance it was tough to project. My plan was to wear my heart-rate monitor and hold this nice, comfortable pace all day. On the bike I learned I couldn't do it, and on the run I learned, again, I couldn't do it.

I saw my cheering section at the top of the first hill out of transition, when I came out of the pit, and then again on Pay and Save Hill. Plus they had etched their encouragements on the pavement with chalk. GO TODD, it said next to my number. It was like the Tour de France, where they paint all the names on the streets. It lifted me up.

Even though I said I would focus on the race, I still felt disappointed I couldn't propose to Lisa. She had no clue, but for me, it was definitely on my mind. I had heard stories about people getting engaged at the finish line, and as I got nearer to it, I knew it wouldn't happen. I didn't have a ring. At the same time, our relationship was so strong that simply knowing she was there—even though she was my girlfriend, not my fiancée—helped me get through. We have such a positive relationship that I draw energy from it.

I've heard people say, "You cannot describe the experience coming down Alii Drive to finish that race." I can't put it into words either, that's for sure, but I know it's powerful, otherworldly. I felt like I was floating down Alii Drive, three feet off the ground, to that finish line. It's overwhelming, and I've never had that feeling again in the four ironmans I've done since. It comes close, but has never matched that first time. I believe part of that feeling is attributed to being on Alii Drive. There's something above and beyond the feeling of accomplishment that goes with any ironman finish because it's Alii Drive in Kona.

The race was over and there had been no major mechanicals, no major medical, it had just taken its course. Everything had fallen into place. I was about seven minutes slower than I was hoping to be—I was hoping to be right at ten hours—but that didn't matter. I finished and it was time to digest it. It was time to let it soak in and realize what the heck had just happened.

I think it finally sank in while I watched other people finish from the grandstands. I felt so good for them that they finished. Then it hit me, 'Man, I did it too. I was just there.' We sat there until midnight, and with every person who was practically crawling in, I realized how fortunate I was to be able to finish strong and that I was able to finish at all. I mean, you hear about the DNFs and the crashes, and I was so grateful for my perfect—almost perfect—day.

The plan was to do only one ironman. I just wanted to try one, that's it, and not even five minutes after the race, I wanted to come back the next year. I'm sure it was the energy of Alii Drive. Maybe all the endorphins in my body were exploding. I didn't think about all the hours I put in to get there and all the sacrifices I had to make—the many things I couldn't do because I had to go train—but finishing made it all worth it.

The whole time there, I kept realizing, 'Man, you're in Hawaii—Hawaii Ironman.' I'd get goose bumps. It was fantastic. It was a dream come true, but it was also dreamlike. It was like being part of a fairy tale because there is so much mystery about Hawaii—there's so much history there. I'd watched many of the previous races on television and just to think, I was out there with people from all over the world who managed to get there and there were twenty thousand other people who tried to get there and didn't. It was dreamlike.

Todd, an environmental engineer in Colorado Springs, qualified for Hawaii the next year and proposed to Lisa two days before the race. She said yes. His cheering section has grown to include two daughters.

WELL-DESERVED BREW

KAREN SMYERS
DATE OF BIRTH: SEPTEMBER 1, 1961
RACE: HAWAII IRONMAN 1993
TIME: 9:21:12

At 4:30 in the morning I was trying to eat my oatmeal. I didn't exactly feel like eating breakfast right then. I was joined by my husband, Michael; sister, Donna; and seven other friends from near our hometown of Lincoln, Massachusetts, all Team Psycho members. We shared a condominium, and Michael and I spent the eve before our first ironman sleeping on the floor.

All ten of us were iron virgins and it was a good distraction to have everyone feeling we were in this together. Even though I was a pro triathlete, my friends all knew I was not fond of this long-distance stuff. Here at the Hawaii Ironman I was a total novice. There hadn't been a Luc Van Lierde yet nor a Natascha Badmann, who did great their first time out. So I was coming to experience it, not really thinking about racing it yet. I was out of my element. We were all walking the plank. We had read in the race program that seventy percent of first-timers underestimate their finish time by two hours. That made us realize most rookies don't have a clue.

We made a video the night before. Everyone separately went

into a room and had to make a prediction of how we would do, what order we would finish. The cocky guys always predictably ranked themselves first. We played it after the race and it was pretty funny to watch them squirm. One thing is for sure, predictions are not meant to be made at ironman.

I had been a triathlete since 1984 and I always swore I would never do an ironman. It just wasn't my cup of tea. I thought those people were nuts—are nuts. In 1991 Michael and I came back from the Australian World Championships through Hawaii just to see it and, oh, what a party! I was very impressed but I also thought it was crazy. I think though, at some point on that trip, I knew I'd have to try it because I realized it was a big part of the sport. Certainly watching the finish line from 11 P.M. till midnight was unbelievable. I started understanding the allure but, still, I hadn't convinced myself I wanted to be a part of it.

Two years later Michael got caught up with trying to qualify because a few of our Team Psycho teammates qualified. A lot of people had just decided that year they were going to Hawaii. There was a qualifier in Boston in July. Michael was going to go for it and I scoffed at him. But I said, "If you qualify for Ironman, then I will too," not thinking he would. Michael went ahead and qualified and I realized I had to live up to my word. I didn't even know how to qualify as a pro. In those days pro spots got passed down a lot. There were a lot of people who didn't want to do it. I had to pull some strings to get Dave Yates [then president of the World Triathlon Corporation] to put up some slots at Mrs. T's in Chicago. One for the men and one for the women. Mike Pigg hadn't qualified either and he wanted a slot too. Luckily I got the one and Mike got the other.

On race morning, after handing in our special-needs bags and checking our gear in the transition area, Michael and I snuck in my parent's hotel to find a bathroom. That's where we said our good-byes. Our goal was to feel good enough after the race to drink a beer at dinner.

Michael's not much of a swimmer, so he planned on starting in the back. I was up front with the pros and had a good swim. It seemed like it took forever, but I wasn't that worried about it because I'm a swimmer. I thought I'd think about seeing fish or sharks, but I didn't. *This is cool, I'm doing the Ironman!*

I finished the swim in fifty-four minutes. Paula Newby-Fraser was a few seconds ahead of me but was never to be seen again. Paula grabbed her transition bag, took out her helmet and went straight to her bike. I went into the changing tent because I didn't know any better.

On the bike I just settled in. I didn't want to push too hard for fear of blowing up. I was being very conservative and watched huge packs of people go by. *Just let them go. You don't want to get caught up in this.* I didn't even see Erin Baker go by. I got passed by several women. I wasn't lollygagging, but I was avoiding going too hard at all costs.

The way I packed my bike looked like I was going on a picnic—I had lots of food. Of course, I hardly ate any of it. Every time I took a bite of an energy bar it would take me ten minutes of chewing and it wouldn't go anywhere. I'd have to spit it out. I just couldn't get the saliva going.

I handed in a special-needs bag for the bike course, but I never got it. I didn't even know when I was supposed to get it. I was prepared to not get it because people had told me not to rely on it. I remember ten miles after the bike turnaround, where the bags were supposed to be, thinking, 'Hmmm . . . I guess I missed it, but I don't know when I missed it.'

I drank what was on the course and managed to get down a couple of bananas and some the energy replacement drink I had with me. I felt sort of sick much of the time. My stomach wasn't being very receptive. Chewing and breathing at the same time is hard to do. Solid food is not the way to go, but I was able to take in semi-adequate calories. Because I wasn't pushing as hard as I could, I managed not to fall apart.

At one point along the bike course I had to take my feet out of my shoes. My toes ached like mad. They had gone numb—a strange sensation in the middle of lava fields—and wouldn't come back to life until I let them out to breathe. It seems like a little thing, but boy did my toes hurt.

I remember trying to pee on the bike and what an ordeal! I'd start the process on a downhill. By the time I'd almost get started, it was time to go uphill again and I'd have to stop. I never tried this training—I just couldn't see myself riding through the streets of Lincoln with pee running down my legs. My mother's biggest fear when I told her we were doing the Ironman was that I'd go to the bathroom on myself on national television. She'd be horrified.

Even though I felt like I took it easy, my bike split was one of the fastest in all the years I've raced in Hawaii. Starting the run I saw the girls who had passed me on the bike. They weren't too far ahead. I felt pretty good, had a nice rhythm, and passed a lot of girls in the first few miles. I was amazed I felt this good. I found myself running my way up to sixth place. My stomach doesn't like running with food in it, so I was convinced I could get by on water alone. I don't know where I got that idea.

Six or seven miles into it I was clicking off the miles—close to a 7:15 pace. I got up to the Queen K Highway and all of a sudden, people I had passed, mostly men, started passing me. I felt like I was winding down. *Oh my god, I didn't train enough. I'm not prepared for this long of a race because I didn't put in enough miles. I have a long way to go. This is going to be hard.* I suddenly slowed down to nothing. At nine miles I started walking and did until mile ten. *This is crazy.*

I knew I would eventually have to switch to Coke. People had told me to wait until the last 10K. But I had to do something right then. I took a cup of it and in thirty seconds I woke up. *This isn't bad.* I felt better and ran. It only lasted for about three-quarters of a mile. I had gone an hour or more without any calories so I was already depleted. I'd see the aid station up ahead, but I'd start winding down before I got there. I'd arrive, have more Coke, and it would get me another three-quarters of a mile. I did this yo-yo thing for the rest of the race. After a while the calories built up in my system and I began to feel better. But then my legs started to ache.

It was definitely hot. I could see the heat rising from the pavement. I looked around at the lava and there was absolutely no shade anywhere. Part of the allure of the race is that it's stark and barren. It's you against the elements. You're naked out there and there's nowhere to hide.

Michael and I saw each other on the bike and the run. Because of the nature of the course you know you're going to see each other. I was definitely looking for him after each of the turnarounds. We high-fived each other on the run. You go by so quickly, though.

I had one big motivating factor, which was my friend Wendy Ingraham, who had done well in past ironman races. She was up ahead. I knew I was probably a better runner although she was definitely more experienced at the distance. *I'd like to get up to where Wendy is.* She was in fourth. I finally passed her around mile twenty-two. I had been doing a little walking but when I could see her it was motivation to keep running. I was able to pass her and I knew once she could see me I really couldn't walk anymore.

About a mile before the finish I caught sight of a motorcycle with a cameraman riding next to someone. It was Sue Latshaw.

That gave me a big spark because she was in third place. I definitely started picking it up and I was closing and closing on her and then the cameraman turned around as he was going around the corner. He saw me coming so he panned back to me. Sue saw that, which was smart. She realized I was coming and sprinted down the hill and managed to hold me off. If the cameraman hadn't given me away I might have been able to reel her in.

Coming down the final stretch on Alii Drive—in fourth place—I realized how well I had done for my first ironman attempt. I knew I was going to go back. It revitalized me because I had been doing short course for so long and this was something new and something I could get better at. It got me excited again about training and I think it helped me with my short course racing. You have to be careful, and it's hard to do two or three long races a year and do short course, but you can definitely do one or two. From then on Hawaii became a big ocus of my season. It's the one race I get really excited about, although I must admit I dread it too.

My parents and I waited at the finish for Michael and Donna, who both arrived a little after eleven hours. In due time we hobbled over to a nearby restaurant for dinner—laughing at our inability to walk. We raised our glasses in a proper postironman toast. We had accomplished our goal and got what we came for: a cold beer.

Karen is one of the few triathletes to master both long-course and short-course distances. She won the Hawaii Ironman in 1995, and five weeks later won the short-course World Championship, making her the only woman to have won both in the same year. She also won the World Championship in 1990, the National Champion title for six consecutive years, the World Cup Series in 1991, the Triathlon Pro Tour in 1993 and 1994, and a gold medal at the 1995 Pan Am Games.

GOLDEN FINISH

Athletes over fifty start their ironman careers.

LIKE SON, LIKE FATHER

BRUCE MURRAY

DATE OF BIRTH: NOVEMBER 15, 1936

RACE: HAWAII IRONMAN 1993

TIME: 12:22:14

I watched my son cross the finish line at the Hawaii Ironman in 1992. I never thought I could do an ironman, but my son insisted I could. "I see a lot of people out there your age," he said. "I just feel like you're in good enough shape that you could do this if you wanted to try it." I knew I could do the swim, pretty sure I could do the bike, but I didn't think I could do the run—the twenty-six miles.

My son qualified again when I was fifty-five and I told him I would try to qualify too. I started training for a qualifier here in Colorado called Evergreen. It's at nine thousand feet altitude. The swim was in a really cold lake and the bike was up a mountain pass. There were only five people in my age group trying to qualify, and there were only two of us from Colorado. I believed I had a chance to win my age group in that race, which I did, but it was primarily because the others weren't used to the altitude.

My biggest concern was that I had never run a marathon. I had trained up to about twenty miles and I wasn't sure if I could get through all three sports—if my body would hold up for the whole day. But I was psyched up for it. My son encouraged me, helped me train, and gave me a lot of advice on what to eat, what to drink, and how often. I broke down the three events and said, "Okay, I think I can do this thing in about twelve hours and forty-five minutes," and that included taking a little bit of a break during the transition periods.

I was anxious about it and certainly felt the adrenaline flowing, but I didn't have any fear. At the start there was a group of people on the beach; a group standing in the water up to their necks; others treading water in front of them; and then the pros. It was a little stressful trying to figure out which group to get into because it seemed the people standing were the ones most concerned about the swim. I didn't necessarily want to tread water for twenty minutes, but that was what I ended up doing. I got into what I felt was a good position. I played water polo in high school and college, so it didn't bother me.

Once the gun shot off, boy, we had all that splashing and kicking. It took probably five, ten minutes to get away from people, but there were still people all around. In my age group, I was first out of the water. I did an hour and seven minutes.

I was comfortable with the swimming because that was my strongest event. I've been in a Master's group since I was forty-five and while I was in the Air Force, stationed in France from 1955 to 1958, I swam for the Air Force Europe swim team. When I got out of the water I didn't feel exhausted. I was already thinking ahead to the bike and concerned it would be a longer ride than normal if I rode with salt water all over my body. I was worried it would irritate my skin. I hosed off in a makeshift shower set up for the athletes before going into the transition.

It wasn't too bad on the bike. I didn't have any flat tires or mechanical problems, but it was hot going through those lava fields—it reached ninety-eight degrees that year. It got hard toward Hawi, where the wind picked up. Then it sprinkled a bit, which actually felt good. The little hill at the end just before the transition area was sort of a surprise. I'd ridden it a couple of times, but I didn't realize after riding for six hours—I think it took me six hours and twenty minutes to finish—that if you didn't change your gears just right, it really was hard on the legs.

I didn't have a special-needs bag. I carried water and picked up Gatorade at the aid stations. I didn't use GU. I ate Power Bars and picked up stuff at each aid station. I usually ate bananas. I tried to eat Fig Newtons, some oranges, but mostly I drank liquids. I didn't eat enough food, but it didn't catch up with me until I started the run.

I never felt like I was going to quit. I never cramped up on the bike. My back got sore leaning over but all things considered, I felt good. The run still troubled me, but at least on the run I could stop and walk if I had to.

The first goal was to finish, the second goal was to finish under seventeen hours, and the third goal was to finish in around twelve hours and forty-five minutes. I kept telling myself, 'The longest this can go on is seventeen hours.' When I got off the bike, I knew I could make it in under seventeen hours.

On the run there are two fairly big hills right out of the transition area where spectators gathered. Having so many people there seemed to make it easier. My wife and my daughter-in-law encouraged me to keep going and not walk. There was a whole bunch of people watching the race all the way through Kona until the lava fields, and that's where I walked—I had to.

Suddenly there wasn't anybody around. I was out there by myself. Then I heard him. "Hi Dad! Keep it going!" My son was headed back in as I was going to the turnaround. He happened to recognize me. I was sort of spaced out.

I thought it was remarkable we were able to qualify. His age group is especially competitive. There usually are hundreds of people competing for one of those slots. But we both made it to Hawaii. It was a big deal. In fact, I had a ring made the year we did it. His name and my name are engraved on the inside. When I pass away, I'm going to pass it on to him.

One of the fortunate effects of taking longer to finish was experiencing the cooler air as the sun set. I got my glow stick at an aid station. It was one of those that you break and—like a wand kind of a thing—you could either hang around your neck or hold.

It was dark as I came out of the Energy Lab. An aid station on the main highway led us back into town. I started getting sick to my stomach, so I sipped on some chicken broth to calm it down. I was really tired of Gatorade about that time. I felt like I needed something different.

I saw all these glow sticks and tried to keep up with them. I ran enough to keep people from passing me. Age groups were marked on the back of our leg, so I kept looking to see, 'Who's in front of me? Am I catching anybody in my age group?' I never did see anybody near my age when I went in.

When I hit town, there were several kids standing at a corner. As the competitors got under the streetlights, they wanted our glow sticks. I passed mine off to a couple of young kids. In town there were so many people cheering, I got a—I don't know if it's a second or third or fourth wind, but something came back. I was able to run the last two miles or so.

My wife, son, daughter-in-law, and some other friends were all waiting at the end. It was a big accomplishment to finish that whole thing and still be able to walk around. We've all seen people collapse and struggle to get across the finish line, but I certainly hadn't pushed myself that hard.

Even still, ironman training is so time consuming and sacrifices so much. When I was working and training, it was difficult for my wife and family because there were a lot of times that we'd want to do something and I'd say, "Jeez, I can't. I have to go on a long run, or long bike."

I'm not sure what motivates people to want to do an ironman, but after doing it myself, I believe anybody with the discipline to do all that training could do one if they wanted to. I don't believe a person could fake it. They might have the desire, but if they don't have the discipline to train, they won't make it, certainly not a person in his fifties.

I think Ironman is one of the hardest things I've ever done. I equate it to being in the Olympics and I think it's by far the biggest event I'll ever do in my lifetime. I have competed in the Senior Olympics here in the United States, but it's not like the Ironman. To me, the Ironman was like I would imagine being at the Olympics would be like. Being in Kona was like being at the Olympic Village.

I have a goal to be the oldest person to finish, and right now, I think Bill Bell at seventy-seven has that honor. If I'm fortunate enough to stay healthy, I'd certainly like to try. I've done two of them now, and they've been five years apart. I'll try another one when I turn sixty-five. Ironman every five years. I think I can get motivated enough to do that.

Between ironman races, Bruce enjoys mountain biking and trail running near his home in Colorado Springs.

SMALL-TOWN GIRL MAKES GOOD

ELIZABETH JOHNSON

DATE OF BIRTH: JUNE 10, 1939

RACE: IRONMAN HAWAII 1989

TIME: 14:59:45

In 1974 I moved from Austin, Texas, back to my hometown of Atchison, Kansas. Population: 11,400. After a divorce I moved there to raise my six children—five boys and a girl. The oldest was thirteen and the youngest was three. It's never easy being a single woman with six kids, but in that era I couldn't get credit and didn't have a car. In Atchison we could get around without a vehicle—ride our bikes and such.

I went to work at the police department and coached an age-group swim team after work. Four years later the YMCA asked me to work for them and set up a swim program. While I was the aquatic director and fitness director, the YMCA membership was mainly men and young kids. Every now and then a woman would come in to work out, but she would do it in the dressing room. Aerobics was starting to come into popularity, so I asked the director if I could get certified as an aerobics instructor, which I did. In the first class I had six people. The next time I offered the class, I opened the door to the gym and there were fifty women there. The next time it was one hundred and the

next time it was two hundred and, of course, I had to break the
classes down. I offered classes morning, noon, and night. The
women of Atchison, Kansas, went through a fitness boom.

The men were having a fit because all of a sudden they could-
n't play pickup basketball in the gym. They couldn't push us
out of the gym because we had hundreds of women paying
memberships to do this and we weren't going to give up the
gym to three or four men for a little basketball. We had taken
over and that was that. Eventually they built us an aerobics
room and relinquished the gym.

In 1980 I got a race application in the mail for the Topeka Tin
Man. (Topeka is about an hour away from Atchison.) I studied it.
I was riding my bike all over town to save money. I swam every
day. I had been running since 1968. I was already doing this
stuff. Maybe I didn't know how to race a bike, but that was the
only aspect of the race that concerned me. Fortunately one of the
members of the Y sold bikes and had raced himself at one time.
He taught me how to shift gears and the etiquette of racing.
From then on I rode thirty miles pretty regularly. I went to that
race and won my age group. I've gone back every year—haven't
missed that race since they started it. I've got a record going.

Eventually I did a half ironman near Kansas City. I did
marathons and other long events and, of course, doing an ironman just seemed like the next progression. I promised myself
I'd do one before I turned fifty. Well, I was busy with my life,
my kids, my work, and all of a sudden I celebrated my fiftieth
birthday. That summer I entered the Texas Hill Country
Triathlon in New Braunfels because it was a Hawaii Ironman
qualifier—my youngest son Dylan drove me to the race. I won
my age group there and the slot for Ironman.

My support crew and my training partners were my children.
The kids all swam, so we were in the pool together a lot. Three

of the kids did track and cross country, and my third son Jere—number four child—used to get up and run with me in the mornings. People talk about how training is time away from their family, but not for us. For several years we used to do a bike rally over Memorial Day weekend, the Cottonwood 200, out of Topeka. We started out the first day with seventy-five miles to Council Grove and then camped out at night. The next day we rode fifty miles, which was down and back from Cottonwood Falls. Another overnight stay and then we'd take off and ride seventy-five miles back to Topeka. We would take the car and two bikes and the kids would take turns riding with me. They would ride about ten miles apiece and then switch out. Of course, we had to work it so we had somebody old enough to drive the car. In the beginning they'd be in a hurry to give up the bike but by the time we got to the third day it was, "Hey, your ten miles are up. It's my turn, get off the bike." I rode the whole way and they just didn't quite understand how I could keep going.

I went to Hawaii ten days before the race to have the opportunity to swim in the ocean and get acclimated to the heat. The first day I did a practice swim, I climbed out of the water and some fellow hollered at me.

"Where are you from?" he asked. "What age group are you in?" He and his wife were there to support a lady who was in my age group and had won it the year before. Of course, he asked me, "Well, how fast do you think you're going to do that swim?" During practice my swim times were an hour and fifteen minutes pretty consistently and it felt good. So I said, "Well, I'm counting on the crowd and the conditions and everything, but I think I'll go about an hour and thirty minutes." He said, "Oh, don't set your sights too high. A lot of people get disappointed."

I had trained and done everything possible to prepare,

including running the soles off my shoes. I came in from a twenty-mile run and the sole of my right running shoe was flapping. I had to buy a new pair of shoes, and really didn't want to. I wanted the old comfort, nothing new going into a race like that. But I had to, which meant making the trek to Kansas City to buy a pair of shoes. I knew a fellow in Kansas City who owned a running store and I called him to see when he was going to be working so I could buy my shoes and pick his brain. I still had a lot of questions about the race. "You know, I might have bitten off more than I can chew," I said. "I'm really scared."

"Well, tell me what your training is like," he said, so I told him.

"Oh, Liz, you've done your homework, now go enjoy the race. The key is to not look at the whole race. Can you swim 2.4 miles?"

"Yeah, I've been doing it every day."

"Can you ride 112 miles?"

"Yes, I can do that."

"Can you run a marathon?"

"I've done four and I'm trained for that right now."

"Then that's all you need to know. Yes, I can. Yes, I can. Yes, I can. You don't worry about how the race comes together because it will. When you're swimming, don't think about cycling. Enjoy the swim. When you get out of the water, unlike in the shorter races, you get out, run through the shower, get the salt water off, and change into some fresh cycling clothes because you're going to be out there on that bike for a long time. When you're out on the bike enjoy the scenery, talk to people, and don't think about running. When you get off that bike, change out of your cycling clothes, put on some fresh running clothes, and run from water station to water station."

The night before the race, I was really nervous. My daughter called and talking to her—because we have such a good relationship—helped significantly. She believed in me.

I tried to stay calm, but my knees were knocking. For years, I had watched the race on television and thought how horrible the swim looked. All those people, body to body, out there at the same time. It was as horrible as it looked. I had scooted clear up behind the pros. The good thing is that the pack carried me longer than I expected and I didn't have to swim that fast. I figured I would have gotten hit and beat even if I was farther back.

I talked myself through it: 'You're okay. You've done this before. You can do it.' And of course I was trying just to think about the swim, and stay relaxed to conserve energy. I battled people the whole way right up to climbing out of the water. People were pushing and shoving to get out. I finished in an hour and sixteen minutes, which was the record for my age group. At the time I didn't know that, but learned later that the gal the year before had done an hour and twenty-five minutes.

I changed into my bike gear and as I came out of the dressing tent, I yelled, "Bullfrog," because that was the name of the sunblock used that year. Three or four women with it all over their hands started slapping on sunscreen. Well, someone put their hands on my back in one place, but didn't get it all over, so I ended up with a sunburn with two handprints on my back.

As I rode up the hill on Palani I saw that fellow and his wife—the one who talked to me on the beach about the swim—and heard him say, "There's that lady from Kansas. She's ahead of . . ." In fact, I didn't see her until about mile forty. As I was out on the bike, I had younger women coming by and saying, "Do you know how far ahead you are?" That was exciting, but it also concerned me because I was advised to not go out hard.

When there was somebody around I could talk to without being in an illegal position, there was a lot of talking going on.

It was hot and windy. I had to come up off my aerobars because I could feel the bike being blown out from under me. I rode leaning sideways into the wind to keep from getting pushed over. Despite the strange angle, I had a decent bike ride.

It felt wonderful to change out of my sweaty bike clothes into clean, dry running clothes. I started running and was amazed—in fact, I ran along giggling because my legs felt so good. I expected they would feel like rubber, or tired, or dead, or something, but I just felt very strong. I was absolutely elated.

The crowds were great and the people were tremendously supportive. It's such a well-organized race. There was a program with all the competitors listed in it—where we were from, and other information. It seemed the aid stations had spotters that would yell to the people ahead, "Here comes Elizabeth from Atchison," and by the time I arrived at the water station, they'd say, "Well, Elizabeth, what can we do for you?"

I didn't feel like a number; they made me feel special. Volunteers care very much that you finish, so they take good care of you.

It started to get dark after my third mile. Volunteers passed out circular light wands. People were putting them on their head and on their arms, and sometimes they'd unhook them and hook them in the straps of their tank tops. It was funny to see someone with two of them hooked to their tank tops. I'd see these two circles coming toward me in the dark and it looked like boobs coming at me. Every now and then, somebody would drop one, and I began a collection. I was pretty well covered by the time I crossed the finish line.

Aid stations offered rolls, and broth, which I wished I had tried the first year. The thought of sitting down and having a bowl of soup didn't make sense. But I have since learned that it really does make me feel better. I ran from water station to water station and, of course, I was very tired. The closer I got to town, the louder the cheering got.

One of the things an athlete must do before attempting an ironman is to strengthen the body core. This won't take a membership to a gym. You can't get it in the weight room. I'm talking body core. You've got to get right with God because you're going to pray out there. I guarantee you're going to pray. And I did; I thought about people who helped me raise money so I could do this race, and my family behind me. I kept going and found all kinds of reasons to finish.

Coming up the final hills I started counting one, two, three, four, five, six, seven, eight, one, two, three . . . and established a rhythm so I could maintain it all the way up the hill. Going down the hill on Palani wasn't as easy as it would seem because although the finish line was in front of me, I had to turn left and run away from it for another quarter mile or half mile before coming back.

When I made the final turn, people were just going nuts. The announcer called my name from the loudspeaker because they knew ahead of time I was coming. As I came across the finish, I didn't know what to expect and if I did, I had forgotten; I was so tired. After I finished, somebody came up and said, "How are you?" And I said, "I'm fine, but I'm tired." This nice-looking older gentleman put his arm around me and walked with me and, of course, I was busy talking to him. I looked at him and thought, 'Boy, he's a good-looking dude. He looks about my age.' Then we turned a corner and we're in the dark, going down a dark street behind this building and I thought, 'Wait a minute. What's going on?' But then we came around the building and there were the massage tables.

I never saw my handsome escort again. A race like that needs to be shared, and none of my kids could afford to come and I didn't have anybody with me. That was hard.

In order to be able to afford to go, I had pancake feeds and a couple of buffalo wing feeds to raise money. The kids helped cook and serve. They were all excited for me. Even still, if somebody mentions the Ironman, they'll say, "Well, my mom did the Ironman twice."

I took pictures and wrote a story for the hometown paper because everybody wanted to know about it. I kept track of who gave me money and mailed a copy of my account to everybody who helped me achieve my goal.

Aside from being an ironman finisher one of my greatest athletic accomplishments is raising children who have grown up to appreciate fitness and include it in their life somehow. The oldest son is at a junior high and high school coaching football, track, basketball, and swimming. Number two son is an off-road cyclist. My daughter is busy raising three kids and she tries to run and swim as much as she can with her family. My third son is a personal trainer and still competes in swim meets and road races. My fourth son lives in Portland and doesn't own a car, so he rides his bike everywhere for transportation. My youngest child keeps saying he's going to get back to swimming. I'm working on him to get back into it.

But there's definitely such a thing as too much. Having trained for and done the race twice, I seriously believe people who do it year after year after year are detracting from the quality of their life. It's very hard on you physically. Of course, socially it's a killer. But when you allow for it, it's an experience to be savored and treasured. This much I know, I want to do Hawaii one more time before I die.

Liz now lives in Dallas and has plans to do Ironman USA. In addition to being an avid triathlete and Master's swimmer, she dances with the Dallas Tap Dazzlers.

IRONVET

NORMAN LAIDLAW
DATE OF BIRTH: APRIL 24, 1946
RACE: HAWAII IRONMAN 2000
TIME: 16:35:27

I went down to the water at 6:55 A.M. and stood on the seashore. The ship we had to swim around was, it seemed, over the horizon. As we were to self-seed according to our swim time, I was in the correct place: at the back. The starting line was about eighty yards into the bay. The cannon sounded and the race started.

My sporting background was not glittering. Swimming was my best sport. I swam backstroke in 1961 for the East of Scotland (once). Then I burst my eardrum and had to stop swimming for a year and never kept it up. The highlight of my sporting career came in 1979 when I was team leader of eight others in setting a new world record for Bed Pushing. We pushed a bed for 3,233 miles, a record that still stands in the *Guinness Book of World Records*. At the Hawaii Ironman I hoped to set my own record—to finish under the seventeen-hour time limit.

Three to four hundred metres out I had a fright when I saw a large dark object swimming underneath me. Fortunately it was not a shark but a frogman taking pictures. The sea was so clear I could see the ground beneath me. I did not see any jellyfish or sharks, thank goodness. One of the athletes later told me he saw a large manta ray glide below him.

Sighting was difficult due to the swells and I must have swum an extra half mile due to all the zigzagging. One of the kayakers had to make me change course at one point because I had sighted on the wrong buoy. I eventually saw the end of the swim and still felt strong. I swam up to the ramp exit and ran to the transition area.

I took my time to dry and put on my cycling gear, and I had volunteers help me apply the sun creams. I had decided to hire a road bike in Kona rather than have the hassle and problems of taking my own with me. I obviously took my own seat and pedals. My rental was a Cannondale 800 with tri-bars and two water bottle cages—I got on and rode away with hundreds of spectators cheering me on. The announcer shouted that No. 863 was Norman Laidlaw from Scotland. On hearing that, I had to get my bum off the seat and show I meant business.

After all, I had something to prove, if for no one other than myself. After having a back operation in 1982 and spending a great deal of time afterward not being able to stand or walk, I decided to keep fit. I took part in a ten-mile charity walk later that year, and the following year I ran a marathon and did so again two years later. But as always happens, I forgot about my pledge to keep fit and slowly put on weight. This caused pressure on my back again and after another operation, I decided that keeping fit for the rest of my life was necessary.

In 1995 I watched the Hawaii Ironman on television and saw an 'old' man in his late sixties complete the event, albeit just outside the time cutoff. This was Bill Bell, who came out the next year and became an official finisher. I said to myself, 'if he can do it, I can do it,' and made it my goal without any idea what it involved, and I am glad I didn't know.

I put off training for a few years until 1999, when I joined the Edinburgh Triathletes on New Year's Day. I didn't realize how unfit I was and how difficult it was to get fit again. My first triathlon was the Edinburgh Millennium New Year Sprint. I was nearly the last person to finish. Not one to be deterred, I sent my Hawaii Ironman application form in and found out on the first of April I had been accepted—was that an April Fool or was I just a fool?

My confidence took a few knocks after racing several sprints in the spring and never improving much over my first time. In July I participated in a sprint triathlon with an open-water swim. I don't know if it was the cold water, even though we all wore wet suits, but I could not get my breath. I even stopped in the water but as soon as I started off again I couldn't breathe. I had attacks of nerves or something. I was told it could have been an adrenaline rush. I really struggled with the swim—no end of the pool to hold on to this time. I was the last to finish in a time of one hour and fifty-nine minutes.

Hawaii was drawing nearer. The mandatory half-ironman distance still had to be completed to confirm my lottery place in the 2000 Hawaii Ironman World Championship. I had to do well in the half ironman, or—the unthinkable—no Hawaii. My girlfriend, Laura, and I traveled to Aberfeldy the day before the race to travel the route. After only eight miles we hit the hill section of the bike route. The car had trouble climbing this hill and as we ascended Laura assured me all the way that I wasn't going to get through it. No way, she said. When the chips are down and people say you can't . . . I will show them.

The next morning I nearly slept in and that would have destroyed me if I had lost by default. I survived the swim—an open-water swim, at that—and when I approached that hill on the bike, I decided to push the bike up and not stop to put on crampons. The other side was obviously all downhill. I am good at that part, that's where the extra weight comes in handy. I was slow on the run but still managed to pass another supervet, and finished third in my category. My persistence paid off. And persistence would be my secret weapon on the Queen K as well.

The bike ride in Hawaii was very hot and windy with side and headwinds all the way to Hawi. In some places the wind was so strong that I had to pedal going downhill to move forward. My only thought was that I would have the wind at my back on the return journey like the elite cyclists I saw coming back. This did not happen for me. The wind changed direction and the slower cyclists were not privileged with that boon. We had sidewinds that gusted up to forty miles per hour. The strong wind also brought showers from the distant hills that made the roads slippy. Not only was I trying to hang on to my bike but also I had to look out for people coming from the opposite direction being blown across the road into me, and the ambulances coming up the middle that were collecting people blown into the lava fields. You probably could not believe it unless you were there.

Everything was cramping up after hanging on to my bike and not being able to drink for fear of taking a hand off the bars even for a second. It was a very long way back with more strong headwinds and endless riding through the lava fields. Every time I got over a hill it was the same again. I was not looking forward to that marathon.

I sweat a great deal and due to the heat I drank about one to two bottles of liquid per aid station to keep fully hydrated. The aid stations were so big (and clear by the time I got to them), I managed to get a bottle of water to douse myself, a bottle of flat Coke, then a bottle of Gatorade and food if I was quick enough.

At the end of the ride my legs and body were all right but the balls of my feet were sore due to the constant pressure of standing and turning the pedals. In transition I took extra time to slacken off my leg muscles before starting the run.

About five miles into the run I went over on my ankle and strained it. The thought of not finishing the race suddenly became a reality. I started to concentrate on a hobble type of fast walk. I was mentally growing all the time; I was going to do it! I was not getting more tired, in fact, I was getting stronger (so I told myself, and it worked). When I reached the Queen K I passed a number of people. The only problem was, they were all going the other way, headed to the finish line. All the time I was growing and not hurting. All I was interested in doing was finishing.

On checking my watch I worked out that I could finish the race even if I jogged and walked it. Another eight miles or so the 'strain' disappeared and I came across Jerry, an American athlete suffering from acute back muscle cramps and thinking of giving up. We talked, exchanged stories, history, and information. This helped us both along.

A mile and a half from town we heard the noise from the crowd at the finish line. We then found the energy to run the last mile and a half. I let Jerry go ahead because I was going to hold the Scottish flag when I crossed the finish. I don't remember much of the last mile—just the crowds of people cheering me home. I finished and there across the line was Laura and my baby Kirsty to congratulate me.

I accomplished my five-year goal—I finished the Hawaii Ironman. What made my finish so amazing were the seven thousand volunteers, the excellent organization, and the spectators, who cheered for me by name even though I was eight hours behind the winner. It made *me* feel like a winner.

I CAN

Physically challenged athletes vie for an ironman finish.

BORN TO RUN

DICK HOYT AND RICK HOYT

DATES OF BIRTH: JUNE 1, 1940

AND JANUARY 10, 1962

RACE: HAWAII IRONMAN 1989

TIME: 14:26:04

Rick Hoyt and his father, Dick, became a team in 1977 when they ran their first race—a five-mile road race to benefit an injured lacrosse player. They've competed in every Boston Marathon since 1981 and finished several ironman-distance races, including the Hawaii Ironman twice. When Dick swims, he tows Rick in a small boat. When Dick cycles, Rick is strapped into a seat, which is attached to the front of the bike. When Dick runs, he pushes Rick in a running chair. Rick was born as a spastic quadriplegic, with cerebral palsy, and the inability to speak. His family has supported his quest for independence and inclusion in community activities, sports, school and the workplace. Rick graduated from Boston University in 1993 with a degree in special education. Dick is a retired lieutenant colonel in the Air National Guard and a friend of the President's Council on Fitness.

DICK:

Rick loves sports. When he was twelve we raised money to make a computer so Rick could communicate with the control of a head switch. It cost five thousand dollars to build, at Tufts University. When the engineers finished the computer and brought it to our house everyone was betting what the first words Rick was going to say. I was saying it's going to be, "Hi dad." His mom was saying it's going to be, "Hi mom." The engineers said, No it's going to be, "Thanks for the computer." Well at the time the Boston Bruins were going for the Stanley Cup and what he said was, "Go Bruins." So we knew he loved sports and was following sports, but he couldn't let us know.

We started attending athletic events with Rick. At a basketball game he was attending, an announcement was made that a lacrosse player had been paralyzed in an automobile accident. He came home that night and told me all about it. He said, "Dad, I have to do something for that man. I want to run in the race." And that's when he asked me to compete. We crossed the finish line and he had the biggest smile I've ever seen in my life. When we got home that night Rick wrote in his computer, "Dad, when I'm running, it feels like I'm not even handicapped." That's what motivates me and inspires me to go out and do as well as I can because of what it's doing for him. He feels like everyone else when he's out there competing.

A lot of people used to get upset with me because they thought I was dragging my disabled son along to get publicity— but it was Rick who asked me to run in that first race. I'm just loaning my arms and legs to Rick. I never thought of competing with Rick as being a disadvantage because I wouldn't be out competing if it wasn't for Rick asking me.

But when we first started running nobody wanted us in road races. We went out and did them anyway. We got turned down for our first Boston Marathon and we got turned down to do the Hawaii Ironman too. Then race chairman Valerie Silk said to me, "You can come and compete, but Rick will have to stay on the sidelines watching. And we said, "No way. We're going to compete together or we're not going to do it at all." We did Ironman Canada and an ironman race in Cape Cod before we were allowed to compete together in Hawaii.

Rick has helped a lot of people become runners and triathletes. And not just people with disabilities, but everybody. It's
not about a disability but living your best life. Our theme is: Yes,
you can. Rick is thirty-nine years old now. For years everyone
said, "No you can't," and now we've proved that "Yes we can."

RICK:

On a rainy day in September 1989 a film crew from a local
television station came to film me at school for the upcoming
Hawaii Ironman, which I would be competing in with my dad,
Dick. The next few weeks flew by and before I realized, the day
to leave had arrived. I had to get up at 4 A.M. to catch the plane
to the fiftieth state.

Dad and I had plenty of support along: Mom, my brothers
Robert and Russell, their girlfriends Mary and Lisa, Russell's
friend Chris, and my personal care attendant Bob. After thirteen hours in the air, we landed on the Big Island of Hawaii.

The next day Dad took Robert and Russell to the airport to
get the boat, the bike, and the running chair. Meanwhile Bob
and I toured Kona. Most evenings we all had dinner at one of
the condos—every two people took turns making dinner for a
night. The following morning Dad wanted to swim the course
with me in the boat and Robert went along too. During our
swim Robert saw a turtle and dove after it not realizing how
deep the turtle was in the water. The rest of that week Dad went
on training rides, while I got used to the heat and began to fuel
my body up with Gatorade.

The Sunday before the Ironman there was a 10K, which all of
us ran. I love competing in races more than anything because it

makes me feel like I'm not handicapped. I am just another athlete and that's how athletes see me. It wasn't that way when we started racing—nobody would come up to me. But soon enough athletes started to interact with us. Now many athletes come up to me before a race or triathlon to wish me luck.

The rest of that week was very busy, between going on training rides, being interviewed for the ABC telecast, the parade of nations, and the carbo-loading dinner. The day before the race I tried to get some rest; however, butterflies kept going though my whole body. That evening Mom made spaghetti and I went to bed early, but the butterflies still were flying. I managed to get eight hours of sleep.

Race morning began at 3:30 A.M. when I got up and took my pills. Dad and I headed to the starting area and got in line so Dad could get marked with our number. A camera crew met us and filmed it. I went to a little stretch of the beach and waited. While I waited, Dad went to check on our equipment, and within ten minutes he joined me.

But it wasn't soon enough. While I was waiting for him, the governor of Hawaii shot the cannon four minutes early. Dad had to take the boat to the water then carry me down and put me into the boat. After Dad put on his towing vest and we got started, the rest of the athletes had a good ten-minute lead on us. This was no problem for Dad—he quickly caught up to the slow swimmers.

At the turnaround boat we were in the middle of the pack and stayed there until Dad and I reached the end of the swim. Dad got me out of the boat, carried me to the bike and buckled me in. Dad also had to put on my helmet and give me some water. Then he had to get himself ready.

Even though this was our first ironman, we had competed in triathlons since 1985. Dave McGillivray (a local race director and technical director at the Boston Marathon) tried for two years to get my dad to do a triathlon. My dad didn't know how to swim and he hadn't been on a bike since he was a kid. Dad kept telling Dave, "No, not until I can do it with my son." Finally Dave said, "Okay, Dick, let's see what kind of equipment you can get." The race was on Father's Day in 1986 and we joke about it being my Father's Day present to him. Dad and I just fell in love with triathlons. When we decided to really get into it, he worked out, up to five hours a day, five times a week, even when he was working. Dad is one of my role models. Once he sets out to do something, he sticks to it.

By the time we got on the bike route, we were dead last. It took a long while before we began passing a few of the other bikers. Hardly any spectators lined the bike route on the highway. When we saw people they were around hotels and at the aid stations, and they were very supportive. The press would come up to us in cars, vans and motorcycles. When we were about halfway to the turnaround, I saw the leaders making their way toward the start of the marathon. A while after watching the leaders fly by, Dad gave me some Gatorade as a helicopter flew over us. The air from the chopper made the Gatorade spill all over me.

As we reached the bike turnaround, Dad and I kept passing a lot of other bikers. Whenever we pass athletes they typically say something like, "Go for it!" or "Rick, help your dad!" I was amazed at where the turnaround was; it was right in the middle of a small village. On our way to the beginning of the marathon we continued passing other bikers, and the Gatorade had begun to mix with my sweat.

When we got to the beginning of the marathon we were somewhere near the back of the pack; however, by the time Dad got me out of the bike and put me into the running chair and got ready himself, we had fallen toward the end of the pack again. But as soon as we started running, Dad and I began to pass other runners left and right.

When I am running, my disability seems to disappear. Out on the road is the only place where I truly feel an equal. With all the positive feedback, I feel people understand that I'm the intelligent person that I am, with no limits.

Around mile six the sun set and we continued to pass other runners in the dark, lit with glow sticks. When we passed people on the run they'd say, "Go Team Hoyt!" or "If not for you, we would not be out here doing this." There were more spectators on the marathon course, until we got back on the highway. But we had the company of the press along. Even so, it was dark and quiet and I was able to think.

When we had 150 yards to go, almost out of nowhere, there was a flood of light and sound, so that I got a little afraid. But once Dad and I crossed the finish line, my fright very quickly disappeared and was replaced by joy. Right after we finished my brother Russell opened a bottle of champagne, which went all over us and the television reporter who was interviewing Dad. I felt very honored to be a person with a disability who completed the Ironman.

To write this story, Rick used a specially built computer with a head switch that selects letters and spells out words. Rick works at Boston College's computer laboratory helping to develop mechanical aids that function using a paralyzed person's eye movements. He also accompanies his dad on motivational speaking tours. The message of Team Hoyt is that everybody should be included in everyday life. "Take time to get to know people with disabilities for the individuals they are," Rick says.

DELAYED GRATIFICATION

CLARINDA BRUECK

DATE OF BIRTH: SEPTEMBER 24, 1955

RACE: HAWAII IRONMAN 1997

TIME: 16:46:19

Clarinda Brueck, a sixth-grade science and physical education teacher in Fairview, New Jersey, is credited with helping establish the physically challenged division at the Hawaii Ironman.

When a podiatrist told me I had run all the fat off my foot bed, I couldn't imagine my life without running. What was I supposed to do? A friend suggested I try this crazy new sport called triathlon. I was born with a congenital defect: my left arm extends only past my elbow, which means I don't have a left hand and part of my forearm. This never posed a barrier for me as a runner, but how do you swim with one arm or set up a bike with this disability?

I decided I'd give it a try anyway at the Wyckoff Triathlon in New Jersey. I was a better backstroker than freestyler and it was only a half-mile swim. Still, now that I look back, it was very courageous—I could have drowned. I did the ride on a clunker bike that was too big for me. I had to create an extension to the handlebars for my left arm to equal the reach of my right arm. I did this by padding a toe clip, attaching it to plumbing pipe, and attaching that to my handlebars with a bike stem. I put both brakes on one handle and my gear shifters on the down tube. I had to balance myself on the extension to change gears. Hills were the most challenging part. I was at the back of the pack, but I did it. When you want to do something, you'll try anything. That was more than ten years ago.

All it took was finishing one and I was off to another one. The next year I began traveling across the country, competing in the Bud Light U.S. Triathlon Series. By now I had a better bike, but my bike mechanic insisted that I ride with my pros-thetic device. He had me positioned so I stayed aero constantly. My adaption allows for my hook to stay in contact with the han-dlebars so I can hold on, but when I wear my prosthetic I don't know what's going on from my elbow to my hook. I can't feel anything, so I can only hope I don't fly out of my adaptation. I had to learn how to ride a bike all over again. I have to balance forces I can't always sense and if the forces are too great, I slip out. Usually I'm quick enough to catch myself but I can easily wind up on my butt.

In 1988 I went to the Hawaii Ironman to watch a friend and training partner compete. The owner then, Valerie Silk, would accept certain requests from physically challenged athletes who wanted to race. That year I watched Dan Leonard, an above-elbow amputee from Canada, compete. He biked the whole course with one arm in that wind. I knew then I wanted to go.

In 1992 I qualified for USA Nationals and spoke to the USA Triathlon president about establishing a way for PC athletes to make Team USA. I wanted to know how I could qualify, how I could make the team. He told me to write a proposal and devel-op rules for PC athletes. I had a fervent belief in what I was doing. I created the guidelines for the division with rules and the whole banana, with a way for every PC athlete to compete on every level.

Two years later, in 1994, I was practically banging my head against a wall to get USAT to ratify the rules and put them in the rulebook. That year USAT was to present a resolution for a PC division to be included at the Triathlon World Championship, at the International Triathlon Union Congress so I made plans to fly to New Zealand, on my own dollar. A week before I left, the USAT board dropped the resolution. I pitched a fit. As consolation ITU let me present a speech on physically challenged athletes. ITU president Les McDonald told me to keep it up. He then named me ITU Paralympic representative.

The next year, in 1995, I went to Cancún for Worlds. I wore my sponsor's colors instead of my country's because USAT still didn't have a platform for me to represent my country. At the starting line I met an above-elbow amputee from Mexico and an above-knee amputee from Italy. We were the first three PC athletes to compete at a Triathlon World Championship and finish.

Finally, in 1996—four years after I opened my big mouth at USA Nationals—I put together the first PC division at the ITU Worlds in Cleveland. There were twelve PC athletes representing six countries.

David Yates, then president of the World Triathlon Corporation, had been watching what I was doing and gave me a phone call. I was glad because Ironman was next on my list. He allowed a wheelchair athlete to compete in 1994—Jon Franks—but he didn't make the cutoff. He was the first to attempt the course on a handcycle and racing wheelchair. In 1996 David Lindsay, a double above-the-knee amputee, successfully completed the course riding a bike with his prosthetic and then completing the run in a racing wheelchair. David Yates wanted to determine how paraplegics and amputees and others with the same disability could compete equally.

We worked together and put something on paper. The hand-cycle division was for paraplegics who could complete the bike course with a handcycle and the run in a chair. The physically challenged division could use a bike and complete the run with or without a chair. In 1997 we had eight athletes at Ironman. Boy, did I get my wish. And that year, John MacLean became the first paraplegic to finish an ironman in an official time. We've been able to give the physically challenged equal competition on an equal playing field with everybody else. That's what is fabulous about Ironman. No other race has stood by what I believe more fervently than Ironman. They stuck by what is right and what is fair.

I was one of those eight athletes—the only woman among them—and I had anticipated that morning for twelve years. I was a little worried. After all, I was the one with the big mouth; I felt that now I had to finish.

My mom was with me the whole way—she was my handler that day. She was able to hold my prosthetic device and see me around the course and give me encouragement as I went from one thing to the next. PC athletes are allowed to have one han-dler in transitions, and handcycle athletes are allowed two because they need to be lifted from the water. The blind are allowed a guide with them throughout the race.

My race didn't get off to a good start—I got seasick some-thing awful and puked twice. I made it out of the water in 2:10. Volunteers took one look at me and escorted me to the medical tent. Dr. Bob Laird, the medical director, took good care of me, stabilized my blood pressure, got me to drink some fluids, and calmed down my stomach. I spent nearly thirty minutes in tran-sition. I was the absolute last person out. Dr. Bob said to me,

"Clarinda, how good a bike rider are you?"

"I'm strong," I said.

"Well, you've got eight hours, you think you can get back in eight hours?"

"Give me my bike and let me go!" And I took off.

I was the only one out there on the Queen K. It was scary. I took it one mile at a time and got to the turnaround. I had wind in my face on the way up and wind in my face on the way back. I worked my buns off. I didn't even know where I was. I stopped at an aid station and got off my bike. A volunteer told me I had only eighteen miles to go and to get back on my bike—I was going to make it. The wind had beaten the living daylights out of me, but I finished with half an hour to spare.

My feet had given me problems on the bike, so I took some time to let a podiatrist tape up my feet while I snacked on bananas and cookies. Race director Sharon Ackles met me in the tent. "Can I run-walk a marathon in six hours?" I asked her. She assured me I could.

I was back in familiar territory. I had started running at age eighteen for the same reason a lot of people start running—because I was getting heavy. I had to drag myself in the beginning. It was, 'I have to run these two miles because I'm fat and I have to lose weight.' As the pounds fell off, I grew to love the solace, peace, and nature I discovered on the roads and trails. I could appreciate the four seasons more intensely than I ever could before. Suddenly it wasn't drudgery. It was a calming addiction. Two miles led to three, then a 5K, then 10Ks led to marathons. Here I was, running yet another marathon.

On the Queen K I had an official adopt me. His name was Don Johnson and he has since become the coordinator for PC athletes. He was checking on my pace and telling me I looked good. He encouraged me to run with this one woman older than me. "You have to stay with her because she might not make it without your help," he said. "Get up there and stay with her and see her to the finish." She wound up finishing before me. We helped each other, though. That's the spirit of the ironman. It hurt a heck of a lot but finishing is like nothing else in the world. As I ran under that banyan tree I felt like I could run another hundred miles. A sense of peace and euphoria all at once. I passed under the finish arch, looked up to the sky, opened my arms, and loudly proclaimed, "I am an ironman!"

Not many people are lucky enough to see their dreams come true. You have to be patient and persevere. I make my dreams come true. There's no better way to live your life.

Clarinda finished the Hawaii Ironman again in 1998. She hopes to put together a team for the Ironman circuit and promote the PC division even more.

I AM IRONMAN

PAUL MARTIN

DATE OF BIRTH: JUNE 21, 1967

RACE: HAWAII IRONMAN 1998

TIME: 11:55:37

Paul Martin had a below-the-knee amputation after a car accident in 1992. He was encouraged to pursue triathlon after picking up a magazine with a picture of professional triathlete Cameron Widoff jumping across a finish line with a singlet that read, WILL RACE FOR FOOD. He figured if Cameron was one of the better athletes and he had that kind of attitude toward the sport, then "It's probably a pretty cool sport."

I slept eight hours the night before my first ironman and I don't even sleep that well for a sprint race. But for whatever reason I was relaxed. I had been in Kona a week already and was set in my routine—feeling good and comfortable. I woke up and had the usual: my daily omelette, PB&J, and a big cup of joe. But it wasn't just another morning. I gathered my things, headed to the transition area, and went through the motions of preparing for the start. It was a powerful feeling getting ready to do an ironman, which made me all the more eager to get on with the day. That feeling, I figured, would only intensify once the race started.

Ten minutes before the start I got in the water and lined up on the left side, per Karen Smyers. At a seminar earlier that week, she recommended that athletes who were wary of the mass start place themselves on the left to lessen the chance of getting nabbed by flailing arms. She said it would only amount to swimming an extra five yards, geometrically speaking. Because I'm not much of a swimmer, I figured the extra distance was worth the peace of mind. It turned out to be a perfect spot for me. I didn't get beat up and the worst problem I had was that my right goggle lens kept leaking. That was probably the only thing that went wrong the whole day.

I knew I'd get through the swim, I just didn't know how long it would take. I wasn't worried about the distance, I had swum the course before and knew what to expect. When I got to the end of the swim my handler, Rich, was waiting for me. He assisted me up the ramp and to my chair where I put on my bike leg. Within six minutes I clipped into my bike and rode off with two legs.

It took me a while to get a leg that fit right. The bike leg is a straight post—straight from the socket to the pedal—with a bike cleat instead of a foot. My power goes straight to the pedal without flexing in the ankle, which would waste energy. As a below-the-knee amputee—my amputation is about five inches under my knee—I still have the same range of motion, but limited knee flexion, so without that foot, I don't have to bend as much in the back of my stroke, giving me a smoother pedal rotation. Riding my bike with this prosthetic is very similar to riding a bike with two legs. Everything is normal, very much in line with being an able-bodied rider.

The best part of my ride was going up Palani Hill—there were so many people cheering. Unbeknownst to me, the announcer called out my name as a first-timer, so all of these people were yelling "Go Paul" all the way up the hill and I wondered, 'How does everyone know my name?' I felt like a celebrity. It wasn't until months later that someone told me people call out names—lots of people's names—because an announcer tells the crowd who's coming. That was a buzz kill.

The ride continued to be great for another twenty miles—until the wind kicked in. The winds were pretty nasty. I could see people ahead of me leaning to the right at about ten to fifteen degrees. I rode at twelve miles per hour for a long time. It was discouraging, but I wasn't any slower than people around me. Soon enough I was up the hills and making the turnaround in Hawi. The best part about Hawi wasn't the prospect of being halfway done, but the opportunity to zip on the flats with a strong tailwind at thirty miles per hour, for a while, until those cursed crosswinds returned.

Earlier that year I had biked across the country in the Transcontinental Triathlon for Life. After 3100 miles of biking I was pretty comfortable on my bike, and definitely had my base training. It took me three hours to get to Hawi and just over three hours to get back to the Kona Surf. I thought I would finish in five and a half hours, but not with those winds.

The way back to town seemed so long compared to the way out to Hawi. The monotony got to me and so did the hills. I thought I was over one hill when right away there would be another and then another little hill. My back hurt a lot, my upper body was sore, and I looked forward to getting that ride over with.

Although I could sense the end was near, my bike computer told me I had long passed the bike finish. When my computer read one hundred ten, I thought, 'Great, I'm about done.' I'm not even sure how I could have had that thought because I knew I would have seven more miles once I got to Kona and I wasn't even *in* Kona yet. That was a drag. I didn't have the wherewithal for mind games. According to my computer, I rode one hundred eighteen miles that day.

I stopped paying attention to my computer altogether once in town. I had a whole different mind-set than when I was on the Queen K for two reasons: It's green and it's populated. At the hot corner I realized, 'Wow, here I am at the big show and I'm almost ready to start the run!' My buddy Joel, another below-the-knee amputee who came along for support (and went on to do the Hawaii Ironman in 1999), was there cheering for me.

In the transition area Rich had my run leg with him and I sat down to change legs. On my way out I saw my friend Susan Lat-shaw, who had earlier bailed out of the race because of a foot injury. She's won Ironman Europe and is a pretty big name in the sport, so to hear her calling my name with a big smile on her face—it was a great way to start the run.

I walked most of the way up the hill out of the transition area then ran down the pit and, halfway back up, started walking again because I still didn't have my legs under me and didn't have my groove going. The pit wasn't nearly as intimidating as I expected it to be, though.

Once at the top of the pit I ran and, with the exception of the aid stations, ran the whole race. I continued eating, knowing I had to eat, even though I wasn't hungry. Mostly bananas and GU, and drank plenty. The sun wasn't too bad, either. I kept on trotting.

Fortunately I had found a run prosthetic that fit better. It didn't hurt too terribly bad. I probably stopped a dozen times at the aid stations to take off my prosthetic and pour ice cold water over Stumpie (it has a name), which felt incredibly good.

When I reached the Energy Lab, I looked at my watch and knew I was on pace to break twelve hours. I was right on. All I needed to do was maintain a 10:30-per-mile pace. My favorite training song popped in my head: Black Sabbath, 'Ironman.'

And in a totally different genre of music, I sang, 'I Feel Good,' by James Brown, over and over and over again all the way back into town.

Before losing my leg, I was a goof-around team player—hockey, football, baseball—never an endurance guy. While I was in the hospital, I had a vision that maybe I could go somewhere with this. I was now different than everyone else, and being different is what makes people stand out. I saw the opportunity in my misfortune. It didn't take me long to get active—I was playing hockey six months later, but I couldn't run on the prosthetic I had. I met a prosthetist a year later who told me he could have me running marathons within a few years. I had to laugh because I didn't want to go *that* far—I would be happy with 5K or 10K. The 1994 National Track and Field Championships for Amputees was my first athletic event and that's where I got wind of Jim McLaren, a below-the-knee amputee like me, who holds records in marathons and the Hawaii Ironman. I figured if he can do what he does, I should be able to go out and do a sprint triathlon without too much trouble. In 1995 I finished a few sprint triathlons and later that fall, like my prosthetist predicted, ran the New York City Marathon.

I cried when I crossed that finish line in the marathon. I was so happy I had run 26.2 miles with a prosthetic leg. I had my doubts I could go that far, but sure enough I did it. It was a moving experience, one I had never felt before, and from then on I pledged to chase that feeling down again.

In the summer of 1997 my father asked if I would ever do an ironman. I laughed. The marathon almost killed me, and I had no desire to go that distance. But by the end of that summer I completed the San Diego Challenge, a half ironman, and it didn't seem as tough as I expected. With that under my belt I applied for the Hawaii Ironman and got in.

When I got to the top of Pay and Save Hill I looked at my watch. Twelve hours was all mine. As I ran down the hill I could hear the crowd at the finish. It was within throwing distance, but the course detours for one last challenge for the day. I hit the corner at Kuakini Highway and turned left, running away from the crowd. I wondered, 'How freakin' long is this stretch?' I turned right again, down another hill, the last right turn, and then, 'Holy shit I'm about to finish the Ironman!' All I could see were white lights, way the hell in front of me. It was probably a quarter mile but it felt like I could make it in ten steps. I kicked it in for the sprint and ran hard—people were going nuts. I crossed the line, pulled off my leg, raised it in the air, and screamed, 'I am ironman!' in true Ozzy Osbourne style.

It was such a glorifying experience to fulfill my premonition from the hospital bed. For sure, running my first marathon was a harder-hitting feeling, deeper emotionally—I did a whole lot more crying at the end of the marathon. The marathon established I could do whatever I wanted. With Ironman, I affirmed it—I reached the goal I set for myself. I could do whatever I wanted to do with a prosthetic. It was empowering, confirming—proof positive nothing can stop me. I can do an ironman on one leg. It was good to see the crowd at my finish and good to have them see me finish.

Paul went back to Hawaii in 1999 and in 2000 competed in the Paralympics in Sydney as a member of the U.S. Cycling Team. He finished fourth in the Kilo, sixth in the 4K-pursuit and seventh in the road race. Paul plans to compete in the Boston Marathon, Ironman Europe, and of course would love to go back to the Hawaii Ironman.

THE MAKING OF A HERO

CARLOS MOLEDA

DATE OF BIRTH: DECEMBER 22, 1962

RACE: HAWAII IRONMAN 1998

TIME: 11:25:55

Carlos Moleda is a two-time Ironman champion in the handcycle division and holds the record of 10:55:58. He coaches track and field for kids in chairs in Virginia Beach, Virginia.

I got into triathlon strictly with the intention of doing Ironman. I saw a segment about the 1994 race and a wheelchair athlete named Jon Franks on an MTV sport video. He didn't finish because he couldn't make the bike cutoff, but it planted the seed for me. A couple of weeks later I read about his race in *Sports 'N Spokes,* a publication for people with disabilities, and decided to give it a shot.

I had been an accomplished wheelchair athlete since I rehabilitated from my injury in 1989. I was a Navy Seal in Panama for Operation Just Cause. We were there to capture Manuel Noriega on drug trafficking charges. Our job was to secure the airport where he kept his jet—his way of getting out of the country. In order to keep him from leaving, our squad had to secure that place and destroy his plane. But the thing was, we weren't in a war against Panama, it was against Noriega and his private army. We couldn't go in and blow things up or shoot people. The rule of engagement is to shoot only if shot at first. So there we were in front of a firing squad and we couldn't shoot. They opened fire and just about everybody in my squad was shot. The guys on my left and right were both killed. It was pretty nasty. I was shot in the back and leg and ended up in the hospital for nine months.

It was a big change for me, real fast. But sport was something that helped me right away. My physical therapist used athletics as a way to get me back into the swing of things. I was lying there in a hospital bed with pins all over my leg and she was telling me, "You're going to do this race and that race." The first time I got into a racing chair there was so much freedom—a regular chair just sucks. I could go fast and far. I could go on forever. I started doing races the moment I got out of the hospital.

I needed to prove to myself I could still do great things and accomplish my goals. It wasn't easy in the beginning, but I realized I wasn't the only guy in a chair. It opened a different world for me.

I became a fairly good wheelchair racer and finished among others, the L.A. Marathon, Marine Corp Marathon, and an ultradistance race—367 miles in my wheelchair. So I had a good foundation in wheelchair racing when I decided to do Ironman. That was an advantage for me because that's one of the hardest things to do.

Before my injury I was a combat swimmer. I knew a lot of strokes from being in the military. But I had to learn how to swim all over again because I never really swam freestyle. I also had to learn how to deal with my legs. I have a small brace that ties up my knees so my legs are straight and makes me plane in the water. With that, I can swim as fast as an able body.

It was the handcycling that I had no idea how to do. It happened that I was good at it once I started because handcycling is less about technique and more about fitness. The way you push your chair in the run is a specific stroke. You have to do it right to be effective and fast. It takes years to be good at it and I had been doing it for six years before doing Hawaii. I was finishing marathons in less than two hours, while wheelchair athletes were finishing in three or four hours. The handcycle, however, was just a matter of endurance. In 1996 I did my first triathlon, the Superfrog Half Ironman in San Diego. That's when I realized I could do Hawaii.

I started to train for Ironman in 1997 and went to Gulf Coast to qualify. The day before the race I got a kidney stone and ended up in the hospital for four days. I couldn't go to Hawaii that year. That was the year John MacLean became the first wheelchair athlete to finish.

In 1998 I went to try to qualify at Buffalo Springs Lake Triathlon in Lubbock. Wow. It was only half the distance and I couldn't imagine how hard the race in Hawaii was going to be. I was one of the last of six guys out of the water, and there were only three qualifying spots. But by mile thirty of the bike I caught everybody. It's not only the distance but also the terrain and the weather that you have to deal with. That race is a good predictor of how you can race in Kona. Especially for the guys in chairs. If they can finish that one, they can finish Hawaii, no problem. I got second place to David Bailey and qualified—I was in.

Just being in Kona was one of the greatest experiences I've ever encountered in my life. It was crazy. The wheelchair athletes got a lot of media attention going in. Everyone wanted to know if the last year was a fluke or if it could happen again. I was so scared of the whole thing because I knew how hard Lubbock was.

Plus I never had gone one hundred miles on my bike and then ran in one shot. I would get home after a ride and be sick. Now I had to jump in my chair and do a marathon? I didn't see how it was going to happen. And I hadn't even done the swim. It was really scary because I didn't know if I could finish, and that was my only goal in 1998.

We lacked so much technology on the hand bikes, yet we had to make the same cutoffs. When I got to Hawaii I drove up to Hawi and saw those hills and felt the wind, and I knew it was going to be tough.

I just couldn't believe I was there. It was a big, long journey that culminated on the beach at Kailua Pier. I jumped over the side of the pier and positioned myself to start. My goal was to get through the swim and have a good bike in order to make the bike cutoff. I was concerned at first when I realized I was the last chair athlete out of the water.

At the ramp two guys picked me up, took me to my bike and put me on the ground next to it. I was done with them for the rest of the day. I transferred myself to the bike and strapped in for the ride.

It was probably good for me to be the last of the wheelchair athletes out of the water. I like to be able to chase someone. It was psychologically easier for me, and at mile fifteen I passed David Bailey and at the turnaround I passed Randy Caddell. I knew I could make the cutoff then and started hammering.

It was amazing. I felt so fortunate to be there. I used to watch Ironman tapes—with Thomas Hellriegel and all the pros—and all of the sudden I was there and those guys are going by me. It was surreal.

The wind was pretty tough. I didn't know how my body would handle it physiologically. The longer I was out there, the better I felt. I had so much energy, I'm sure just from the excitement. Toward the end of the marathon I had escorts following me telling me I was on record pace.

When I was going down Palani to get to Alii, I started to cry. I realized I was about to finish a goal I had initiated two years ago. People were screaming for me. It was a dream come true.

I ended up breaking the record by more than an hour from the year John MacLean first announced to the world that an ironman could be done in a wheelchair. It's still new territory. We still don't know how fast we can go on a good day. We still have a lot to learn about training. After all, we do everything with our arms.

Finishing Ironman helped me become a better person, and a better athlete. And I realize how much hope it brings to kids in chairs. There are people with disabilities who were born like that. They don't have athletes to look up to because they can't relate. They can't relate to Michael Jordan or Michael Johnson because they can't dunk a basketball or run. When they see guys like me doing the ironman it's something they can look to and believe they can do anything.

All these events I do for myself, but there are people around me who feed from it and it encourages them to get out there. Breaking these barriers broadens their horizons.

Carlos has finished the Hawaii Ironman three times and plans to do Ironman Europe with hopes of breaking his own record. After completing Hawaii Ironman 2000, Carlos greeted his wife after her first ironman finish.

THE EARLY YEARS

Ironman finishers between 1978 and 1983.

HEAVEN IS A RAINBOW SNOW CONE

BOB BABBITT

DATE OF BIRTH: MAY 5, 1951

RACE: HAWAII IRONMAN 1980

TIME: 14:28:33

Bob Babbitt is the publisher of Competitor *magazine, based in California. Since his first ironman in 1980, Bob has remained close to the event as a participant (he has competed in the Hawaii Ironman six times), race announcer, and chronicler of the sport.*

In 1979 I read an article in *Sports Illustrated* about this thing called the Hawaiian Iron Man Triathlon. At the time, I was rooming with Ned Overrend, who would eventually become the world mountain bike champion, but back then he was working at San Diego Suzuki wrenching motorcycles. We both thought the race sounded pretty cool and decided we were going to train for and attempt the event in 1980.

I was a schoolteacher in 1978, running a PE program. I was playing six hours a day with kids. I played elbow tag and capture the flag and kept my heart rate up at about 170 all day long, so I was good for short-distance stuff. But I had no idea if I could finish this event. In fact, I didn't think the race was in one day. I thought it was a two-day event. I thought you swam 2.4

miles, rode 56, camped out, rode back the next day, and then you did the run. So I had panniers on my bike with my sleeping bag and tent. I was sort of surprised when I got to the island. "You do it all in one day?"

Ned and I trained in the pool at our condo—not a real pool with gutters and stuff. It was maybe twelve yards long. Whenever some fat guy jumped in the water it was like being caught in the middle of a tidal wave.

The pool was 120 lengths to a mile, so we did 240 lengths. I got through by counting in tens, but who knows how many we ended up swimming. We would get dizzy. We'd get out of the water and stagger on the deck.

I bought a bike from a police auction. It had been in a fire and cost me sixty dollars. The whole back end was burned and I immediately bought a fuzzy raccoon seat cover, added padded handlebars, and had a Radio Shack radio mounted on top. I didn't know how to change a tire, so I bought solid rubber tires. I actually waxed the tire rims to get them on. And my training rides were never longer than thirty miles.

In February Ned and I flew to Oahu—the last year the race was there—and the funniest thing happened when we got there. Gordon Haller, the guy who'd won the race in 1978, had a big ol' beard. He was a guy from back East. I had a big ol' beard. There were all these Navy Seals on our flight who were going to do the race, and they saw the guy with the big ol' beard and thought I won the Ironman. We got off the plane, and they rolled out my bike with the solid-rubber tires and the fuzzy raccoon seat cover and the radio on top. They thought that was the bike that won the Ironman. They were looking at it like they were checking out Greg LeMond's bike.

In 1978 fifteen people had started Ironman, and fifteen people started in 1979. In 1980 there were 108 of us. It still wasn't like there was some huge crowd doing this thing. In those days, you had a support crew and the course was the Waikiki Rough Water Swim in the big waves, the Around Oahu Bike Race, and then the 26.2-mile Honolulu Marathon. There were big storms on the island, and ABC called the race director and said, "We're over here for cliff diving and that's on Sunday. If your race is Saturday—the way it's supposed to be—we'll come and film it, but if you have a weather delay of some sort and you have to move it to Sunday"—which they had done the year before—"we're not going to film you." So the race director made a decision to move the swim to Ala Moana Channel.

There was a meeting with all the participants to let us know this and before the meeting started—before we knew the swim would be moved—Ned and I stood on the veranda of this hotel, and nine-, ten-foot waves were breaking up against the veranda. Ned and I just looked at each other. "We're going to die. We're never going to get out past the breakers."

After the announcement, all of the real ironman guys were saying things like, "What a bunch of pussies! I can't believe that!" I mean, Dave Scott is in there and Rick Kozlowski and all these Navy Seals. Ned and I were happy . . . we would live.

There was a guy in the race named John Huckaby, fifty-nine years old, from back East somewhere. He was sponsored by some vitamin companies and wore a jacket with THE INCREDIBLE HUCK on the back. Huck's claim to fame was that he was an ultra-marathoner. He had run the Athens Marathon three times in a row—back to back to back—seventy-eight miles in one day. But he couldn't swim a frickin' stroke. Our swim was four laps in the Ala Moana Channel. I was swimming in a shallow section because I wasn't very confident. On my way back on my first lap, I almost ran head-on into this guy's knees. John Huckaby was walking the swim. He walked 2.4 miles—the only guy ever to do the swim and get blisters on his feet! Later in the race The Incredible Huck was lost in downtown Waikiki in the middle of the night. Race officials had no idea where he was. They didn't have a time limit back then, and he decided to stop in a diner for breakfast. They spotted him coming out, wiping his face off with a napkin. So it was a little different crowd than you see nowadays.

After my swim I met up with my support crew. One of the kids I taught, her dad lived in Honolulu and volunteered for the job. He had a little Fiat convertible, and he and his two girlfriends decided it would be fun. First job was to get me ready to ride. I had socks that came up to my knees and my Jack Purcell tennis shoes and my wool cycling jersey. I didn't know what to eat during something like this, so I had given them twenty loaves of Hawaiian sweet bread. I got on my bike and tuned my radio as I rode through Waikiki. The station played back a Rolling Stones concert from Maui. I was so jazzed. It was unbelievable. I rode through Waikiki thinking, 'What a great experience.'

Twenty-five miles into the ride, I saw my support crew on the side of the road. It was like we were going to do a Tour de France handoff. "This is so bitchin'." I rode along and reached out, and they handed me a Big Mac, fries, and a Coke. At mile seventy-five they got me a snow cone, a rainbow snow cone.

I was riding along, sight seeing. I had never been to Oahu before—it was an adventure. Just that morning, I took the panniers and sleeping bag off. I finally realized I had to do it in one day. But I was twenty-eight years old. I could do anything.

I've always been halfway decent in heat. I think I'm good at self-preservation, and I don't really race these things. It's all about survival. I like playing the mental game of 'everything is a positive.' It's all little power dots. So as you're swimming along, it's not, 'Oh, my God. I'm only halfway to the turnaround.' It's,

'Bitchin, halfway to the turnaround. That's great. I'm almost halfway done.' Everything is a positive. Five miles into the bike it's not, 'One hundred five frickin' miles to go.' It's, 'All right, there's only twenty-two 5s in 112 miles . . . and one of those is done.'

But at some point on the bike it hit me. 'We are way out here.' And when the wind was howling I thought, 'Jesus, this is bad.'

The ride ended at Ala Moana Tower and as I pulled into the little transition area, I heard this touchy, feely music coming from a boombox. I looked over and saw bamboo mats laid out, and there was my support crew. I got off the bike and put the kickstand down.

"We think you should lie down and have a massage."

"Sounds good to me." So I lay down and got a forty-five-minute massage before starting the marathon.

They had a rule back then where they weighed you every five miles. If you lost five percent of your body weight, they pulled you out of the race. I was eating my Hawaiian sweet bread and drinking water and Gatorade and whatever else they were giving me. I got to the first aid station and stood on the scale. When I got to the next one, I heard the guys on walkie-talkies going back and forth.

"Can you repeat that?"

"Yeah, he's at 154 pounds."

"One hundred fifty-four pounds? At the last weigh station he was 151. This guy's gained three pounds in five miles. How can you gain weight? You can't gain weight during this race!"

I felt pregnant with all that Hawaiian sweet bread and water and Gatorade and my rainbow snow cone. Oh, and my Big Mac and fries.

Because I was walking so much I never felt that bad. I don't remember being in a lot of pain during the run. But Ned was a different story. Ned's wife-to-be, Pam, was his support crew. She's not the most aggressive person in the world, and this is Waikiki with horrendous traffic. At eighty miles into the bike, Ned hadn't seen her. He was stopping on the side of the road drinking out of sprinklers. He ate nothing out there the whole day. I still remember when I came back to the hotel that night and walked into the room, the moon was coming through the window, and there was Ned's back to me and his back was the brightest red I've ever seen in my whole life. He just rolled over and said, "I didn't see her all day long."

I, however, was pampered by my crew, gaining weight as I went along. About mile twenty of the run they were following behind me in their Fiat with their lights on, which was really cool because it was pitch black. There was nobody out there. I was running along with these headlights behind me and it was almost like I was leading something, like I was the star of the show.

I came into town and saw a little line across the road with a wire overhead and a lightbulb hanging from it. I slowed down and stopped at the line.

"Hey, you," I heard this voice in the dark and looked over.

"Yeah?" I said.

"You in the race?"

"Yeah."

"You're done!"

Where was the brass band? Where were the big crowds? Where was the big ironman hoopla? I walked over in the park, and there was one idiot doing one-arm push-ups and some other guy doing sit-ups. There was a whole collection of wackos.

'This is the stupidest thing I've ever done,' I thought.

The worst part was the trophies. One of the reasons we did this thing was because it was called the Ironman, right? The manager of Nautilus Fitness, who was putting the race on, thought 'Ironman' was insulting to the women, so they changed the name that year to the Nautilus International Triathlon. So here we are expecting to get this bitchin' trophy of this metal guy with the hole in his head and they give us a seashell mounted on a plaque. How anticlimatic is that? I wanted to be an ironman. I didn't want to be a seashell boy.

That was ironman number one. I've finished six and the race has come a long way in twenty years.

The main difference between then and now is that it originally was an adventure. I didn't know, Ned didn't know, we didn't know what we could do. We really didn't. I equate it to the wheelchair guys. When they started in Hawaii no one knew if a wheelchair person could do this. Could they do it at all? Could they do it in the time limit? Finally, in 1997, a guy named John MacLean finished within the time limit. In 1999 Carlos Moleda went 2:19 in the marathon, finishing in 10:55. His time would have won the race overall the first two years. That's what I like so much about the wheelchair athletes. It brought ironman back to the roots of, 'Can I finish?'

One of the funniest things I hear now is, "I had a bad race. I had a bad day." Maybe they finished twenty minutes off their time or thirty minutes off their target time or an hour. None of us ever had target times. John Collins started this event and his son, Michael, did the race in 1979. Michael Collins was out there more than twenty-four hours doing the race. I interviewed Michael and I said, "So tell me about your day." He said, "Well, I'll tell you, you know what a bad day is? A bad day is when you're walking in the marathon and you're walking through town, and you see the paperboy and he's delivering the paper with results of an event that you're still in. That's when you know you're having a bad day."

That's what you learn from this event: what really is good and what is bad. I think things don't change. Technology is different, but the deal is athletes still have to swim to that buoy, then they've got to get to Hawi on the bike, and they've got to run back to town. The same things are true for them that were true for us. It's you against you. Everybody shares that— whether you're a pro, a competitive age-grouper, or just out to finish. Anybody who's done this race feels an immediate bond when they meet somebody else who's done it . . . it's a lifetime bond. It's like that snow cone. Every time I have a snow cone now, I compare it to the one I had at mile seventy-five of that race, and there will never be a better snow cone, ever.

So for these athletes now, there will be a point in their race when someone hands them a sponge that's the best sponge they ever got, or someone will hand them a peanut butter and guava sandwich that is the best thing they've ever tasted or a cup of Gatorade that's chilled just perfectly or an ice cube that goes under a hat and it's the best feeling in the world. To ironman athletes, that ice cube—in one-hundred-degree heat, twenty-two miles into the marathon—is the best gift they have ever received. While some of you will be sitting around the house thinking, "God, this couch is uncomfortable and my remote isn't working very well."

Bob taught until 1984 and then jumped into the magazine business, working for Running and Triathlon News *until 1987, when he helped launch* Competitor.

INTO THE MYSTIC

SCOTT TINLEY

DATE OF BIRTH: OCTOBER 25, 1956

RACE: HAWAII IRONMAN 1981

TIME: 10:12:47

photo by robert oliver

Scott Tinley has competed in triathlon as long as the sport has existed and is considered one of the legends of triathlon.

I had been doing these short races in San Diego over on Fiesta Island, inside Mission Bay. There were maybe two or three triathlons a year from 1976 through 1978. One of the guys who was doing very well in all the events—Tom Warren—owned this tavern where I hung out and drank beer sometimes. I didn't know him well, but considered him kind of a rogue. I saw him at a race the summer of 1978 and asked him about his training. He was very obtuse about it, as he still is. He said, "I'm going to do a race in Hawaii and it consists of this, this, and this," and I go, "Oh, yeah, right."

Part of why I didn't take him seriously was because I hadn't even heard of it. It had happened for the first time that year in January and the word wasn't out. That was my introduction to ironman. Ironic, isn't it? I didn't even believe it existed!

Warren raced Ironman the next February, in 1979. I was attending college at San Diego State and when I came home from school one day my roommate said, "Hey, you should read this article in my *Sports Illustrated*." I didn't get *Sports Illustrated*. I never read those magazines. "It's about that guy, Warren, who owns Tugs Tavern, and it's about triathlon." I remember, to this day, taking that magazine and sitting down and reading the first paragraph and not being able to put it down.

The author was a guy named Barry McDermott. He was an incredibly gifted golf writer for *SI* and was in Honolulu to cover a golf tournament. Somehow he convinced the *SI* people to let him stay an extra week and cover the race. He was compelled by it all so he wrote this 4000-word, lyrical, and moving piece that spoke to my heart. It took me an hour to read it, and as soon as I finished I said to myself, 'I gotta go.' Then I started reading it again. I was infatuated by the whole thing. This guy, Warren, whom I knew, and this race, which I had heard about, took on a mystical form for me.

I talked to Tom about it that summer and when fall came around I started thinking about signing up. But then I became more of a realist. In 1980 I was in paramedic school and was completely overburdened. Being in a classroom eight hours a day didn't leave much time for training. Besides that, I couldn't afford to go to Hawaii.

But when I began working as a paramedic I had all this time off. Then the race came out on *Wide World of Sports* in 1980. For some reason, it was one of those kismet things again where I caught a glimpse of it on television—the last three minutes or something—and I thought, 'Okay, I really need to do that next year.' I was training a lot more because I had this radical schedule, working only ten days a month. I was racing every multi-sport race I could find, which again, at this point, was maybe five races, but I wanted it, so I made plans to do the Ironman in February of 1981, the first year they moved the race to Kona, on the Big Island.

Two weeks before leaving for Hawaii, I took a new job, which I thought was a great opportunity at the time. I was managing a marine recreation facility where I had taught when I was an undergraduate. The whole deal was shaky. I'll take this job, I thought, but I need to do this one race, and I need a week and a half off only two weeks after starting the job.

Miraculously my boss gave me the time off. I remember thinking. 'Okay, I'm only going to do this once so I'm going to do a little bit of training for it because it's going to cost money we don't have.' My wife, Virginia, and I were newlyweds and had just bought a little house. It was a big deal for us to go to Hawaii, but I still felt pulled very strongly toward it.

Virginia bought me a new bike for my birthday the month before the race, and it was a very expensive deal—a real splurge. It cost $189 for the whole thing, an SR Grand Course, which to me was totally state of the art. It weighed twenty-eight pounds, but I thought it was pretty cool. It was much better than what I had before, which was basically a rusted-out, converted beach cruiser. I usually borrowed bikes for races because I couldn't afford a real ten-speed.

When we landed at the airport—Kona's airport was this ten-foot-square stand—we took a cab to our hotel. We were driving where the Wal-Mart is now, but back then it used to be the dump, although we didn't know that at the time. They were burning trash and all this smoke was coming up. To show you how green we were, my wife says, "Look Scott, there's the crater and it's smoking." I didn't know for sure, but the guy driving the taxi was laughing so hard. He wouldn't tell us one way or another.

We stayed at this tiny place for thirty dollars a night. It was a closet. I laid all my stuff out the night before thinking I had everything. I had my touring shoes with the straps that go over the top, my wool shorts with the big chamois in the bottom, and then, to stay cool, I had this big cotton tank top that was more like a parachute. There wasn't a rule, but I wanted a helmet anyway so I had one of those Skidlids. Remember those? It was basically foam rubber with a piece of polyethylene plastic over the top of it. Actually, it didn't even connect to the top. It was the weirdest thing. The only other options were the leather hair net, which didn't do a thing, or those big Bell Tour Lights, which were like turtle shells. I had all the stuff out and I was sure I was ready. I could not ask for any more stuff, perfectly satisfied in my selection.

Still, there were no expectations. I knew I'd done okay in some of the shorter races in San Diego, but it had no bearing on what I was trying to do, mainly because it was an entirely separate thing. I was intimidated by the swim because it was so long. I was okay in the ocean having swum a lot as a lifeguard, but I knew I wasn't that strong. I ended up swimming 1:05, which I thought was slow because I had seen the times before, and they were just over fifty minutes. As it turns out, the course was measured wrong and even the fastest guys came out barely under an hour.

In transition I changed my clothes and put Vaseline on—only because Mark Montgomery told me I should. I had seen Mark at a couple of races in San Diego and, to me, he was everything because he had done Ironman the year before, in 1980. He knew all about it so he told me all these little secrets, which really didn't amount to much. But I looked at his bike, and he had a big handlebar pack with a map of the course on it and a big glass jar of peanut butter inside, and I thought, 'Okay, you're the expert.'

I got on the bike and I remember thinking, 'Oh, this is kind of fun.' Then it got really arduous and my attitude turned to 'I want to get off this stupid bike.' Fortunately, in 1981 they still made us get off our bikes to weigh ourselves. I stopped, I weighed myself, got back on, and on the way back, had to weigh myself again. In Hapuna we went out to this cul-de-sac, up to the parking lot, up to a cabin, and got on the scale. It was great to get off the bike. I liked those little breaks. By the last twenty-mile stretch, I hated everything about the bike.

Volunteers had all sorts of things at the aid stations and I ate my share of peanut butter and jelly sandwiches. Just recently I was talking to Tom Warren about the early days. He said, "Do you remember peanut butter and jelly sandwiches? If you look at all the nutritional things now, that was the absolute best thing you could eat: carbohydrates, low fat, low protein, it tasted great, you would digest them, you were used to them." We washed them down with ERG—electrolyte replacement glucose—the thing to drink back then.

It was developed by a high school science teacher in San Diego named Bill Gookin. They used to call it Gookinade, and the only place you could buy it was from Bill's garage. We'd go to his house in La Mesa, east of San Diego, and buy Gookinade by the pouch. I had bought my own Gookinade and mixed it up, but they had it on the course. He had shipped over a couple of cases. They don't make it anymore, but it's a pretty good formulation. He was a smart guy way back then.

When I got off the bike I changed into this outfit that was going to be *the* thing—cotton running shorts. I didn't feel like I was running that fast, but I passed so many people. Later on, I found out I'd passed something like fifty people. I ran 3:19, but at that time, even though I was only running about 7:50 minutes per mile, everybody else was walking, running, walking, running, or just running nine-minute miles. It was cool to pass all those people. We made the turnaround in the airport, got weighed again, and went back out to the Queen K. I thought, 'Oh gosh, I might be in the top ten.' Then I saw this guy—the first guy coming back—and he's a tall, gangly-looking guy running right by a cameraman. It was John Howard with a quirky little bike hat right out of the movie, *Breaking Away*. About twenty minutes behind him, firmly in second place, was my friend Tom Warren.

I realized I didn't remember John Howard passing me on the bike. Somebody might have gone by for a second, but 326 people over fifty-six miles—you just don't see people. At one point I could look—as far as I could see—not a soul, not a car, not a cyclist, not an aid station, not one damn sign of life and I turned around and looked back, and it was the same thing. I thought, 'How barren and desolate is this experience?'

I ended up placing third and to this day it was the most exciting finish of my career. Placing well was completely unexpected. It was innocent—I wasn't prepared for it, wasn't in the mindset. In fact that was the only year I took my surfboard with me, which says a lot. That rawness left me with a greater capacity to feel more emotion for what I had just accomplished—much more than I was ever able to feel in the ensuing years.

Scott went back to his job at the marine recreation facility but only for a year. He returned to Hawaii the following year and won, going on to compete in more than four hundred triathlons, winning nearly one hundred of them, including the Hawaii Ironman again in 1985. He was inducted into the Ironman Hall of Fame in 1996. Although he continues to race, he is equally well known in the triathlon community as a writer, scholar, poet, and philosopher. And, when he does race, he takes his surfboard.

MORE TO EXPLORE

LYN BROOKS
DATE OF BIRTH: MAY 20, 1948
RACE: HAWAII IRONMAN 1981
TIME: 12:42:15

After completing her first ironman in Hawaii, Lyn Brooks returned nineteen more times.

W hy don't we do Ironman?" One of my training partners suggested it after a bunch of friends finished a race that started in York, Pennsylvania, and finished in Baltimore.

We all said, "What's Ironman?" He told us, and we thought he was on drugs. But for whatever reason, I began to tell people, "Oh, I'm doing Ironman, ha, ha, ha." The conviction in my voice started to change and gradually it was, "I'm going to do Ironman." I didn't know what the hell I was doing. There was nobody on the East Coast or from around here who had any knowledge of it or even had any interest in training. And I wasn't sure how I was going to manage it financially. But just as the conviction changed in my voice and my inner self, things just unfolded so I was able to go.

I had friends who stepped forward in support. This one woman said, "I'm writing all my friends, and they're going to have to pitch in." So here came checks for, literally, ten, fifteen, twenty-five dollars. And people sending in the checks were saying, "I'd like to see if you could do this."

When I look back through the years at some of the things I've done, other than Ironman, I see this whole concept of buying into something. When I said, "I really want to do this," it became part of me. It's really phenomenal how the universe kind of opened up in a way that allowed it. I didn't see it that way then. I had a lot of maturing to do, but that ownership and the belief that 'Yeah, I'm going to do this,' I had without realizing it. It's conviction. When I choose to do something, there's no half ass. It's commitment. And by the way, none of my friends, including the guy who suggested it, went with me to Ironman that year.

I biked outside once. It was a fifty-mile ride with a friend and we ended up lost way out in the country, freezing. I had to knock on somebody's door because the sun was going down. "Can we wee-wee in your house? Where the hell are we?" The rest was literally sitting on the stationary bike down at the fitness club. I'd sit there for two hours in a row pedaling away, and the club members would come and go and we'd chat some, but I would stay right there. I went to the pool, and I thought, 'Okay, so I have to swim 2.4 in Hawaii. I wonder if I can swim three miles?' I got in and swam three miles just to make sure I could do it.

I did my first marathon—the Maryland Marathon—in 1976. So that was under my belt. I was playing a lot of racquetball and doing a lot of road races with some long distance in between. I was fit in running, but the other two . . .

The race was February 14, Valentine's Day. It wasn't even called Ironman back then. It was the Nautilus International Triathlon. Valerie Silk and her husband owned the Nautilus center in Oahu, and they sponsored it. I came in on the fourth year, which was the first year it moved to Kona—to the Big Island. They had held three on Oahu and my understanding is when it reached one hundred participants, officials on the island said, "Look, this is getting too big. Go find another place." I don't know whether that's true, but that's what I've always heard.

My father dropped off me and my friend Flo at the airport. I had my bike, one of those forty-pound clunkers with the four brakes up top. What did I know? I wheeled it in with my bags and my bike—not boxed, not anything.

"Hi, my name is Lyn, and I'm going to Hawaii. Here's my bike."

The airline gal said, "But you have to box your bike."

"Huh?" It never even dawned on me.

We didn't have any tools, and my dad had left, but the baggage handlers helped out. It was very frenetic. We ended up taking pedals off, rotating handlebars; they stuck it in some plastic bag. It was wild.

We arrived at night so the whole drive to the hotel was in the dark. We woke up at the Kona Lagoon—it has been closed for years now, I swear, it's not because of us. I was there only three days before the race, not understanding that I should have been there much earlier.

I was overwhelmed and intimidated because of my perceptions. Everybody was fit. Most competitors were from the West Coast. They all had suntans. I had never seen Lycra before. Here I was going to do the whole event in my running shoes, my two-tone green-with-yellow-ribbing gym shorts, and an Izod tennis shirt because I could put the collar up and cover my neck a little bit from the sun. That was what I was going to wear until I saw everybody else.

I got on the phone. There were maybe two bike shops in the

area—Kona has changed drastically in twenty years. None of them had any bike clothes. I called a bike store on the other side of the island in Hilo, and they had one pair of wool bike shorts left. I had them mailed overnight to Kona. I sat in the receiving area of the hotel waiting for the truck to come.

As race day approached, my anxiety climbed. The day before I was really scared because now there wasn't a buffer day between. Tomorrow was the day. I was lying in bed saying, 'I'm sick. I can't swim. I don't want to be here. I can't do the race.' My friends have finally made me realize I've done that every year for twenty years. I wake up and suddenly I have a psycho-somatic ache or pain. There are pictures of me with ice on my neck and shoulder. I just knew I had a pinched nerve. I couldn't even turn my head. I mean, extreme pain. I would say, "It isn't in my head, godammit, look at me." Race morning I'm always fine. Sometimes I'm a very slow learner, but now I understand and really believe in an ability to store those stupid things in our tissues.

Race morning I was petrified. It was this big, unknown adventure and this long day, but once the gun went off, I settled in. I wasn't afraid of the water at all. Even to this day, one of the joys for me when I've gone back is to swim by myself, way out into that bay, take my goggles off, look at the mountain, and appreciate this tiny little spot in this big, big world. That's always been a precious thing for me to do every year—I love that water and that place.

The bike was interesting because I had never been on a bike that long. My butt and the bottoms of my feet, especially biking with running shoes, felt like somebody was jabbing them with ice picks. My bike time was a little over seven hours. Even as I became fitter and knew what I was doing and had better equip-ment, I only improved my bike split by thirty to forty-five minutes the following years.

They scared us to death about dehydration. It seemed the race had as many aid stations as they do now, certainly not as massive, but we carried a lot of our own food. I had one of those old-fashioned bags, the ones that would clip on the back with two little hooks. I moved it around to the front somehow so I could have access to enough food to feed the entire number of participants out there. I had three peanut butter and jelly sandwiches, oranges, I think even a banana or two, some candy. I packed for war.

We had to get off the bike to be weighed about three times during the bike course. If we lost more than seven percent of our body weight, we would have been yanked. I had been scared so much about dehydration that I drank lots of replacement drink. Every time I got on the scale, I got heavier. I gained seven pounds by the end of the event. I felt like the doughboy. Eating, drinking, retaining everything.

I had never before biked and then run. After getting off the bike I had somebody rub my feet for a long time. I was notorious for taking forever to get out of the damn change tents. I think I spent twenty-five minutes in there.

I clearly remember telling myself, 'I will run this.' I started to run. 'Well, this certainly isn't going to work so I'll just run until I have to walk.' And then I kept running. But this was my thing and I had prepared for it.

On my way down Alii Drive back into town before the highway, my lower back was killing me. Flo was with me and we went into a fast-food place that is no longer there, and asked if anybody had aspirin. I got what I needed in there, but I'm not sure if it made me feel any better.

Back then the run turnaround was in the airport. That's how slow the island was. We could go in through the airport right down the airport drive, around the circle, and come back out. The airport was three little huts. Kona had one stoplight.

Near the end Flo kept yelling at me, "Pick it up. You're only five minutes behind." I was approaching town so I had five miles to go. "Pick it up, pick it up," she said. And I was going as fast as I could and I didn't care who was in front of me or how close they were. "Pick it up—only five minutes behind!" Finally I turned to her and said, "Fuck you."

Coming down Alii Drive I was just elated. I was ahead of where I thought I would be and happy the day was over and very happy to be able to shed the anxiety leading up to it. I think when something is new like that, no matter how bad it feels, you somehow put it in a positive place. I always forgot the misery very quickly and that's one reason I kept going back.

Finally I came across the finish line. I had changed out of the Izod into some T-shirt, had my green shorts on and my running shoes, everything was drenched. I ran the marathon in just over four hours. One of the volunteers approached me like he was going to have to hold me up. I was annoyed and said, "I'm fine. Get away, I'm fine."

I was third that year and I knew I was going to get a trophy. At the Kona Surf Hotel, which was the headquarters then, they kept the trophies in a glass case. Before the race I looked in there and said, "That is the ugliest thing I've ever seen." And I won it—third place. On the way home I walked through the airport holding my trophy like I was the cat's meow. I wouldn't be caught dead doing that now. That ugly thing became very, very precious. Now I think it's one of the finest trophies I've ever seen. It's one I will relish for a very long time.

When I finished it became very clear to me, right away, that I needed to go back. There was more to explore. But I didn't go into it with a statement of, 'I'm only doing this once,' or, 'I'm going to do this for a long time.' I just went and I did it. I had no agenda. This whole twenty thing was never planned. There was an ornery part of me that almost dropped at nineteen just because it's a pissy number. My friends were saying, "You can't stop at nineteen." "Well, yes I can. You go do twenty if you want."

Throughout those twenty years and my entire life really, sport has been the platform for my change and growth. To me ironman is a level playing field in terms of the physical. Yes, some of us are very slow, and it's people like us who make people fast, but we're all prepared in our own way. But what is very different is who we are and how we handle the obstacles that come our way. Yes, it sucks and yes, it hurts, but how do you get to the other side of what is put in front of you?

I think some of the tough times in these events have made me realize my boundaries. My limitations are so beyond what I thought they were. I've learned patience. And I've learned to appreciate more. That's why I ask people, "Were you happy with how you did in the event because I don't care about the times. Were you happy? Was it satisfying?" I think when you go back to numbers and times and places, you set yourself up to fail or to feel like a loser because chances are whatever plans you lay out, they're not going to play out that way. I've seen so many people train so hard and then they piss the whole experience away because it wasn't what they wanted to do. It's not how fast or how slow, it's just, are you present? Are you appreciating the fact that you have a healthy body that gives you the privilege of doing something like this? I am very appreciative because I also know it can turn on a dime—on a dime.

It has been wonderful to have done ironman as many times as I did, but I've found it is just as wonderful to not have it on my mind anymore. I was reading something in *USA Today* about a woman who was going to her first one and blah, blah, blah, and at the end of the article it said she had gotten in through the lottery, and I went, 'Whoa. That lottery came and went. I never even thought about entering.' Those who are obsessive about it can't believe it's really that way for me now, but it is. Other things—time for other things. Don't you think twenty is enough?

Lyn recently moved to a country home where she is constantly entertained with a parade of wildlife. She has a private practice in massage therapy and teaches at the Baltimore School of Massage. Without another ironman to train for, she fills her time with gardening, birdwatching, and, as always, staying fit.

AGING GRACEFULLY AS AN IRONMAN

BILL BELL

DATE OF BIRTH: NOVEMBER 19, 1922

RACE: HAWAII IRONMAN 1982

TIME: 14:34:49

At seventy-seven Bill Bell became the oldest ironman finisher in May 2000, when he competed in Ironman California. He was fifty-nine when he finished his first ironman.

I stood on the shore of Kailua Bay, with the pier to my right, and I thought back to earning my swimming badge as a Boy Scout nearly fifty years ago. I grew up around the beaches of Los Angeles, and passed many a summer day swimming from pier to pier. The distance was about a mile. Before I got this wild-hair idea to do Ironman, though, I couldn't swim five laps without stopping.

The long ocean swim was just like my mind and body remembered and I had plenty of time to mull over how far I had come to that day as a fifty-nine-year-old man facing the biggest physical challenge of his life.

The first two to three hundred yards I was kind of hyper. My breathing wasn't right and it took a few minutes to get my rhythm going. I watched my stroke beneath the warm, blue water. I watched my wedding ring move away from my body as my left arm reached forward, then watched as it came back toward my heart. Margie, my wife of thirty-five years at the time, was on the shores waiting for me to return.

The swim start then wasn't bad—with seven hundred or so people. Now with fifteen hundred, it's terrible. The start of the swim can be the worst part of the race. You just get beat up. Triathletes are very good to other triathletes, except in the swim. If they go by you on the bike, they say, "How you doing, you're looking fine, hey I'm passing you." On the run it's, "Everything okay? You need anything?" On the swim it's, "Screw you!" But that year I didn't get the beating I'm used to now. I definitely have more anxiety now than I did then. The older you get, the more you start thinking about all these things, especially: 'Will I make the time cutoff?'

I got out of the water after what seemed like an eternity, but it was only an hour and forty-seven minutes. I put on my wool bike shorts and rode away on my brand-new, $125 Nishiki. That sounds like nothing now, but you have to understand, I had never paid more than twelve dollars for a bike in my life. A friend of mine had got me a 'deal' on this bike and when he told me how much it was going to cost, I almost had a heart attack. I was so proud of it, though—you know how bright and shiny brand-new bikes are. Fortunately he had the wherewithal to tell me to get rid of the kickstand and the reflectors, which I did reluctantly.

The victory for me was in participating in such a strenuous athletic event. My father died when I was fifteen. Instead of going out for the football team, like I so badly wanted to do, I worked to support my mother. I was a paperboy and lawnboy. I mowed, edged, watered, cleaned flower beds for thirty-five cents. And that was the front and back lawn. I didn't have the thrill of sports as a teenager and when I wear my finisher shirts now, it's like wearing my letterman's sweater—fifty years later.

In 1942, during the Big War, I wanted to enlist in the Army Air Corps. My eyesight was not 20/20, so I couldn't get in. Next I tried the Army's Airborne Division. I made it as far as the physical, but the doctor said he couldn't let me in because I had a bad heart. I was devastated. What I would give to have words with that doctor now.

There was a lot of wind on the bike ride. My feet were strapped into the birdcages on the pedals and I pulled and pushed my way down the Queen K Highway. I liked the out-and-back course because I could see my competition. There were a couple of people behind me, which was a thrill. You always like to know you're not last. The aid stations weren't anything like they are now, but I took in my share of bananas, cookies, Coca-Cola. They even had greasy doughnuts on the course.

I didn't even know enough to be afraid of bike problems. But you always worry some. You worry about a flat tire, you worry about a broken chain, you worry about a broken spoke. These are the things that happened to me during training and I thought, 'Gosh, what if that happens during a race?' And of course, it did.

With just forty miles to go, my chain broke. Back then they didn't have people out there to help with mechanical problems and you couldn't take aid from anyone. I never rode without my chain breaker tool though, so I settled in to fix it. I'm an engineer by profession, and putting a chain on is no big deal. But as I was fixing the chain, the tool broke. I asked ten cyclists as they rode by if they had a chain breaker. Eight didn't know what it was and the other two said no. This one fellow in a car stopped and wanted so badly to help me, but I didn't want to take the aid for fear of being disqualified.

"Here, let me just give you these pliers," he said.

"No, I can't take any help," I told him.

"Then let me just throw them on the ground, and you can pick them up."

It was tempting, but I didn't even want to do that. I just put the chain back on as it was, but I couldn't shift. Later I was going up this hill and thinking how hard it was because I couldn't put it in an easier gear, when this other cyclist rode up from behind me and said, "Hey, do you know you have a flat tire?" Oh jeez! I pulled over and started to change the tube. Even though the passing bikers were probably going only ten miles an hour, it felt like they were whizzing by like stock cars. I worried I was losing valuable time. In a desperate attempt to get going, I put only fifty pounds of air in the tire.

It wasn't two miles later that I broke two spokes. I had to get off the bike and disconnect the brake. I managed to ride in and I saw Marge sitting on the balcony of our room at the Kona Surf.

"Where have you been?" she said. I had been out on my bike for more than eight hours. "Don't ask," I said. "And if anyone wants to buy that damn bike, sell it!"

That was my start. Since then I've only had three flats in seventeen races in Kona. So luckily, I think everything happened at once that first race. If you think about it, the swim is all you, the run is all you. The bike is, who knows? Will the tires stay up? Will the chain stay together? There are a million things that could go wrong and sometimes do.

Once I got into the run and looked at the clock, I knew I could make it. I had on a pair of gray gym shorts, tube socks, and a pair of running shoes that were too small.

For me the worst part of the race is the run. I'm not a good runner, never was a good runner. In high school I was scared to death in gym class that I'd get on the coach's nerves and he'd say, "Okay Bell, four laps." That was only a lousy mile! And here I am running marathons now.

Back in the 1970s I had a stress test and the doctor detected what that Army doc must have found. He told me the best thing I could do was run three times a week for forty minutes. After the second week I asked him, "Can I run every day?"

In 1979 I read about Ironman in *Sports Illustrated*. The next year I watched it on television. At the time I was traveling a lot as a vice president for my company and on our way to Taiwan, we stopped in Honolulu. I saw a guy with a race T-shirt from the 1980 Ironman. I couldn't stop talking to the guy about it, and I knew then that I wanted to do it too.

Every year it's just like the first year. But it's worse now, because you know what's out there. You remember how much the wind blows, you remember that terrible twenty miles up to Hawi. You remember that last hill you ride up before you get off the bike and then you think, 'Oh my God, twenty-six miles.'

Even back then, as small as the race was, I could see the lights and hear the crowds as I approached Alii Drive. Margie was waiting for me. I finished my marathon in just under six hours. She worries about how hard it is. She still doesn't understand why I do this. I finished. It was anticlimactic, not like my finish in 1995 where I kept falling and was bleeding all over the place.

In those days race results were antiquated compared to today. The only people who really knew what happened were the front-runners. That was the year Dave Scott, Scott Tinley, and Tinley's brother were one, two, three. Three days later I called the race office from Los Angeles. "Can you tell me how I did?"

The lady said, "What age are you?" I said fifty-nine. I told her I finished in 15:57:48. Then she asked for my number and I told her.

"You were third in your age group," she said.

"Oh! You're kidding?"

"Yep," she said, "you were third."

"Oh, I gotta go back! I gotta go back and do it again!"

The standard retort is, "Well you've done it once, isn't that enough?"

I don't think so. Certainly not for me. My brother died at seventy. He smoked, drank, and was overweight. My dad died at sixty-five of a heart attack. I'm doing something right. My blood pressure is 117/76. I have a teenager's blood pressure and I'm not taking any pill. My brother-in-law used to eat greasy food and smoke cigarettes and tell me, "You're going to kill yourself doing this crazy-ass triathlon stuff." Well he's been dead seven years.

Triathlon changed my whole life. My day starts anywhere between three and four in the morning. I do my rowing exercises, my ab workout, and stretching. I go swimming. I come home and have breakfast with my wife. Then I get on the treadmill, or go race-walking, or I get on my bike, either my Computrainer or the road. And I just feel good. Being in triathlon is addicting.

Bill and Margie are retired in Indian Wells, California. Bill says he hopes to get a few more ironman races out of his system.

AROUND THE WORLD

Stories of first-time races outside the United States.

SURVIVING

TERENCE SWEE

DATE OF BIRTH: JULY 14, 1972

RACE: IRONMAN MALAYSIA 2000

TIME: 15:25:05

May 28, 2000. This was the day I was re-born an ironman. For five months my whole life centered on this day. Every weekend was spent doing the time on the roads in Singapore and Desaru. Every lunch hour was spent running in the sun or swimming in the pool. Was I prepared for the ironman?

I contemplated the distance when I was on the plane to Langkawi. That's when reality hit me. On small island Singapore, this was like swimming around Sentosa, cycling to Malacca, then running from Tuas to Changi Airport.

I awoke at 3 A.M. to imbibe my first shot of complex carbohydrates. My stomach felt bad. I scrambled to the toilet and shitted my guts out. I decided to stay away from solid breakfast.

Two hours later I was up for good, although I hadn't slept much since I was up last. I took another shot of liquid carbo. I awoke my girlfriend, Weeguan, while I was giving my transition packs a once-over. I showered in steaming-hot water to warm my muscles and improve blood circulation before stretching. I then lathered a thick cream of sunblock all over my body and went out into the cold morning air to take the coach to the race site.

On arrival, I proceeded to check in my transition bags, locate my pre-checked-in bike, and pump the tyres. I attached my Jet-stream, strapped on all the nutrition I carried for the bike leg: four energy bars, concentrated Ultra Fuel, ready-to-drink Ultra Fuel, four packs of Power Gel, five tablets of guarana extract energy booster pills, and four salt tablets. After making sure everything was in order, I asked Weeguan to put her signature on my bike as a lucky charm.

At 7 A.M. I was off to a good start, finding a sweet spot behind a male swimmer. We were to do two laps of 1.9K. After the first round, I realized I could go faster than I was going so I moved ahead hoping to catch the draft of the white-capped profession-al five metres ahead. I pushed forward and managed to catch her, swimming at her feet until the turnoff. I already had con-served enough energy to go it alone for the rest of the swim. The swim finish banner was in sight. I started to tell my blood to stream itself to the legs rather than the arms. I rehearsed in my head the transition routine. Jersey before helmet, socks before shoes . . . I came up from the water in a respectable time of 1:06. I wondered if the course was short.

After a reasonably quick transition, I got onto my Zipp and started the 180.2K bike leg. The route took us two rounds of 70K along the coastal roads of Langkawi and then a 40K loop right into the mountainous heart of the fabled island. We all had heard from the national cyclists the horrors of the ten-storey climb that awaits us in this loop. I had tried it twice in the three days preceding the race. I was psychologically prepared.

I checked my heart rate once I got onto the main road at Kuah Town. One hundred sixty-seven beats per minute. Too high. Must be the adrenaline rush of the transition. About ten minutes later, once out of town, I relaxed and took out my first energy bar. Before I could finish it, I hit a road bump and dropped it. I was somehow grateful. Soon after, my alarm went off alerting me it was time to eat again. This happened every fifteen minutes.

I was traveling at thirty-seven kilos per hour. I needed to go an average of thirty to hit my target time of 6:30 and I was well on target. The first hills appeared and I took it all in my stride, passing eight persons in the process. This gave me a rush. It was going to be a long solitary ride. I reckoned I deserved some entertainment.

I knew there would be a series of three hills to climb so I popped a booster pill, knowing its effects would kick in when I came to the hills. True enough, the caffeine in the pill pushed me up the hill pretty painlessly.

The first omen of trouble started here. My stomach began bloating up. My alarm went off for a feed. I relaxed, took out a bar, and started chewing. It tasted terrible. I had trained with this stuff, but I guess it's different after having seawater in your mouth and trying to eat in thirty-three-degree heat. I force-fed myself and promised myself no more bars for a long time.

I finished the first 70K loop in 2:21 with an average speed of thirty-one kilos per hour. Ahead of target. However, I started feeling the effects of not eating those bars. I could feel my energy level slowly bleeding away as I turned the pedals. I headed out on my second loop. This was the one that would kill my appetite completely. I had ignored my meal alarm for three cycles, each time postponing the prospect of having to eat. I turned to gel instead. As I only had four packs of gel, not intending to rely on it totally, I knew it wouldn't be enough for the remainder of the ride. 'Gotta eat the bar,' I thought. I started choking on the bar and spit the last mouthful out. No way. My stomach hurt. I was hoping my Ultra Fuel would provide enough carbohydrates. At each aid station I took water to dilute my concentrate. I searched for my salt tablets. Not in the pocket. The isotonics provided at the aid stations were so darn diluted. There was not going to be enough salt. Hyponatremia slowly set in. My quads started to feel slow and fatigued.

I watched my speedometer in desperation as my hard-earned average began to dwindle to thirty kilos per hour, then to twenty-nine. I managed to keep it there for some time. I had not arrived back at the hills yet, which I knew would bring the average down more. To make matters worse, it started pouring; the fast downhill stretches had to be done with less speed. I started to pedal harder, but my heart rate would rise above 160, which was not something I had planned for. The fast stretches had lots of cross wind too, something that didn't happen during the course inspection. I rode on my disc wheel while nature played this cruel joke on me. I swayed down the narrow road, trying not to fall into the drains at the side and to avoid cattle dung.

I remembered there was a right turn at the Burau Bay Resort. I came to a junction that kind of resembled it. There was no marshal there, but then again, there were a few turns before this that weren't marshaled, so I took the turn. It wasn't until a villager caught up with me on his motorbike that I realized I was on the wrong route. I wasted 7K and thirteen minutes. In a 226K race, what's a mere 7K? I soldiered on, glancing at Weeguan's signature at the side of the bike.

Back on the race route, the people I had so painfully passed were now way in front of me. I managed to catch only two Taiwanese on their fancy carbon bikes.

I finished my last pack of gel and I knew my game was up. The ten-storey climb loomed ahead. I stood up and hammered away slowing at one point to just seven kilos per hour, but employing a completely different set of muscle groups. I slowly powered up the slope.

After that my system went into glycogen deficit. I was hungry but couldn't eat. My stomach bloated up so bad I had to loosen my race number belt. My speed started dwindling and I just couldn't pick it up. I had two chain runs that took about a minute each to fix and I stopped twice to pee. I finished the bike leg in 7:06—still on target for a sub-fourteen-hour finish. But that little voice in my head told me, 'No way. You have not eaten anything for the last three hours and you have a 42.2K run ahead of you. Are you joking?' I recounted. I could do it. I kept reminding myself that a human body has enough fat stored to run two marathons back to back. (This, of course, is not physically possible as the fats cannot be metabolized completely, but it was convincing enough at that moment.)

In the bike-run transition tent, I knew I had hyponatremia. My legs immediately seized up into massive cramps. My shoulders were so stiff I couldn't even lift my arms to take off my bike jersey. Bending down to my shoes made my toes cramp. Luckily there were masseuses in the tent to relieve the cramps in my calves. After a pretty long and painful change in the tent, I struggled out to face the marathon. I tried to go into a slow jog, taking in some liquid carbohydrates that I had prepared in the run bag. On leaving town, my stomach just gave way. I ran into the fire station ahead and shit my guts out.

I continued on and passed George Chong, a physical fitness instructor from Hwa Chong Junior College. Barely three hundred metres down the road I had to go again. This time I was near the stadium and got into a toilet there. My intestines were all twined up inside. After a good stretch from the squatting, I continued and got into a comfortable pace of about 6:30 per kilometre. I was planning on running the first half marathon at about 2:15.

By the time I reached the 10.5K turnaround, I had shitted

five times, doing it in the bushes at the side of the road, using the icing sponge to clean myself. At about 13K I could feel my face, hot and red. I knew then I was suffering from the heat. At about 17K I had double vision and everything was a blur. This was the first time I actually experienced delirium and double vision from heat injury. I knew I must drink up even if it made me shit more. It was either drink-shit-finish or heatstroke-collapse-DNF. I chose the former.

I started myself on Coke, alternating with isotonic. I shitted twice more. By the time I got into town, the pain was unbearable. I couldn't feel my toes anymore and my legs felt like two giant trunks of wood. Tears welled up in my eyes. This was not the way I wanted to do an ironman. I wanted to finish in style and comfortably, not struggle. This was too cruel. Five months of training with almost no social life, no weekends. It wasn't fair. I kept crying in pain as I entered to the transition for the turnaround. I checked my watch; it was 6:20 P.M. I had been going for almost twelve hours, the last six without food. I spotted Weeguan. She noticed I was crying. I told her it would be a long day for her and not to expect me back till way after my personal target of 9 P.M.

My first triathlon, seven years earlier, also took longer than it should have, but not for the same reasons. I was just slow, overweight, out of shape, couldn't run for nuts and hardly a swimmer. The Olympic-distance race took three hours and fourteen minutes. The year before, in 1992, while I was in the Army doing my national service, I was fielded to do the cycle leg in a relay. After that first race, I was so hooked on the sport I made a vow to come back the next year and do the whole thing. Now, competing in an ironman, I was discovering what the whole thing was about.

I struggled step by step out of Kuah Town and into the hills

again. By this time, a lot of people had started walking. The toll
of the day was being felt all over. I made another attempt to run. I
managed five hundred metres each time before my whole system
threatened to shut down. I relented and slowed to a brisk walk.
My head was spinning from the heat. I took shelter in a bus stand
and decided to take a five-minute nap. I was so afraid I would
wake up in a hospital bed that I ended up not falling asleep. My
heart rate was below one hundred. I toiled on. Each time an
ambulance passed me, they slowed down and eyed me with suspi-
cion. To prevent being stopped for a medical opinion, I gave them
the thumbs up and managed a smile. I knew if they were to take
my blood pressure and weight then, I would surely be removed
from the course as I was on the verge of a total collapse.

Night fell and the next turnaround was still nowhere in sight.
I toiled on. By this time I was managing a little banana at each
station. I had to ask the volunteers to peel the bananas for me.
My fingers were numb and not responsive.

I kept going with only one thought on my mind. I want to be
an ironman. Mr. Yee Sze Mun, sixty-three and a four-time
Hawaii Ironman finisher from Malaysia, passed me. "Even if
you walk to the finish, you still will be an ironman." Daniel
Yap, a leukemia survivor and a three-time Hawaii Ironman finisher from Singapore, passed me. "Whatever you do, don't
stop!" How could I let these people down? Then there were the
supporters from Singapore. Friends, some of whom I got to
know just two months ago, flying all the way up with us at their
own expense, standing out there for the last fourteen hours,
braving the sun and rain, taking photos, cheering us on. There
were Jean, Colin, Harn Wei, Mrs. Hoong. For them, the race
would not be over when it was over. They needed to help us
pack, retrieve our bikes, maybe even carry us back to the hotel.
They would be out there longer than any of us. There were 1000

volunteers out there doing the race with us. They had been there since 2 A.M. preparing. And then there were the village children who came out to cheer us on.

All these faces played through my head as I opened my stride and walked toward Kuah Town. On the last leg after the turn-around, I stopped by every aid station and thanked all the volunteers and medics there, as that would be the last time I passed their station. As the lights of the town came into sight, I began to jog. It was painful at first but then my muscles warmed up. I couldn't stop. If I did, my whole body would cramp up. I pushed all the way to the line. Luckily, a traffic police started pacing me, slowly revving his bike at my snail's pace. I felt like a president. We made our journey through Kuah Town. Traffic stopping at all the junctions just for me to cross. I couldn't afford to do a side-step or stop. My legs seemed to be able to go in one direction only.

The finish line came into sight. I picked up the pace. My legs cramped but I didn't care. Everything was a blur. I had so much tears in my eyes I couldn't see clearly. Someone passed me something. It was the Singapore flag. I held it up above my head proudly with my last ounce of strength, causing my shoulders to cramp as I headed straight for the coveted ironman finish.

The moment I hit the line, everything happened very fast. Several people caught me as my legs crumbled under my weight. I was escorted to the medical area where I was given a drink and put on a bed. I felt near death, but I survived the ironman. It was painful, but then, if it were easy, it wouldn't feel so good.

I will definitely do this again.

Terence Swee is a research scientist in one of Asia's leading high-tech incubators. He also is an accomplished musician. During his postgraduate days he played gigs at local hotels to save money for his first bicycle.

ONE OF US

T. J. MURPHY

DATE OF BIRTH: SEPTEMBER 18, 1963

RACE: IRONMAN AUSTRALIA 1998

TIME: 12:43:40

The starting gun went off and, the weirdest thing, I couldn't hear anything even though I saw water splashing, people yelling, and a helicopter hovering over Forster Key. The mixture of sounds rolled into white noise that became difficult to register over my own thoughts. I was nervous, but knew good old butterflies were essential; it meant I would be putting my heart into the race and getting something out of it as well. I took my first strokes as the sun started peeking over the trees, lighting our way for the two-loop swim.

I don't think I swam farther than a mile in training, so 2.4 miles, considering my lack of confidence in swimming, seemed like somebody who wasn't a runner going out and doing a marathon. I had no idea what it was going to be like, but knew I had real trouble swimming in a straight line and what I didn't need was to make it longer. I'm certain if somebody put a tracking device on me and did some sort of digital overlay on a course map, my path would have looked like a lightning bolt. I'd think I was going the right way, and suddenly I'd see a kayaker staring down at me like, "Dude, the race is over there, man."

Swimming has never been a strength because I rarely work hard at it. That's probably one of the reasons why triathlons are something I try just to finish. Sure, I have time goals, but mostly I race to experience it and enjoy the training up to it and enjoy the fun afterward. I've always taken running more seriously, probably too seriously at times considering I was never a pro athlete. In triathlon I like the soul of the sport, the people who are part of it and the international mixtures. It's an incredible way to meet people, and then get to experience a place like Australia.

Forster is a great town. It's like going back to the 1950s. The way they dress, the pace of life, tiny shops owned by people who live in Forster with families that have always lived in Forster. It's one of those towns that wraps itself around a race.

One of the reasons I chose Ironman Australia was because my downtime as a triathlon magazine editor is the winter, when I wasn't traveling to races to cover them. This gave me the time I needed to train and do the race in the spring, before triathlon season started heating up. Everybody says, "Oh, man, I would love to have your job. You get to travel to all these races." Yes, you do. You sure do. You travel and you get to the hotel, then you figure out the course so you know where to go. You're also the photographer, as a matter of fact, because the magazine can afford only one ticket, so you run around with your camera and your notebook and your tape recorder, and you don't get a single workout in the whole weekend. Then you fly back and you put the issue together, and you feel this building guilt because you haven't trained in days. You actually gain angst toward the sport in a weird way. As much as you love triathlon and that's why you took the job—you can't pursue the sport yourself. To use a high school football analogy, you're part of the team, but when the team wins, you don't feel part of it because you don't have any dirt on your knees. Everybody else has bloodstains on their jerseys, and they're bathed in sweat; you've been shivering the whole time sitting on the bench. That's a good analogy for how I ended up feeling.

I was hanging out with extraordinarily fit people—icons of physical fitness—and I was out of shape. I had always been fit—in fact my best marathon was 2:38—and not being fit bothered me because I knew how good it felt to be peaked and racing, and how great it felt after the race, that sense of relief in achievement. But there I was, feeling like a blob.

As editor of *Triathlete* magazine, I was a supportive component of the sport, and it's very cool to do that. It's a privilege, but at the same time, I didn't want to be on the outside anymore. I had been with the magazine for about four years when I knew I had to do an ironman somehow or another. I convinced myself I could cover the race and compete too. When I cover a race I watch the best I can, but the story really depends on postrace interviews. I figured I was doing better than watching the race because I was actually out there; not only was I getting what might have happened up front, but I was actually following the leaders' tracks, so I got a real look and feel for what they had to go through.

The bike course was a two-loop course and as I came to the end of the first lap, I thought, 'Gawdang, my knees are hurting.' But I forgot about the searing pain as I rode into town because I was waving to everybody, with little Aussie kids cheering for us. But as I left town, my attention moved back to my knees. They were on fire. 'Jeez, I've got to talk to a coach about my position on the bike.' I was certain I had my seat height the same, but finally I looked down at my knees. 'Whoah!' I checked the angle of my knee during the pedal stroke. My seat—like an elevator going down—was now sitting on my frame, and my knees were sticking out like airline wings. 'What am I thinking? I'm the editor of *Triathlete* and I can't even set myself up on my bike? This is pretty pathetic.' It was the stupidest thing I had ever seen. It was like I was riding a tricycle. I followed the line up my leg to the seat bolt and realized I didn't tighten it enough. And I didn't have an Allen wrench with me.

I had learned at the pre-race meeting that volunteers in yellow coats were mechanics. Of course, I had to find them. My knees were screaming. I stood up as much as I could but felt like they were already damaged.

The course is measured in kilometers, so course markers were practically meaningless to my racing mind. Even though I took chemistry and can do metric-to-mile conversion, I was tired and all I knew was 10K equaled 6.2 miles, and it pretty much ended there. At any rate, I biked along for another half hour and people I had passed long ago were flying by, looking at me pitifully. "Hey, good luck," I'd say. "You got any Advil?"

Finally, like a vision from God, I saw two yellow-coated people. "Are you guys mechanics?" I asked as I pulled up to them.

"Yes, we are. We sure are. You having a mechanical problem?"

"Yeah, do you have an Allen wrench?"

"What's an Allen wrench?"

I took a minute to describe it and they did indeed have what I was looking for. "Please fit, please fit," I said as I approached my seat post. And it did. Everybody talks about how moods can change drastically in an ironman. I went from utter despair to pure giddiness. In fact, I was in such a good mood I wanted to chat. "I love Forster," I tell them. "You guys have a great little town and a great race."

"Oh, thank you very much, mate."

"What do you do?" I ask.

"I'm a car mechanic, actually."

"That's wonderful." I beamed at my new best friends.

"As a matter of fact, mate, if you take that wrench and turn it the other way, you'll get a little more leverage."

"How about that," I responded. "That's great."

We went back to talking about Forster and I was tightening, tightening, tightening, blabbing away, and I heard, 'Crack!' I had overtightened the bolt to the point of destroying it.

"You don't have a bolt, do you?" I asked the car mechanics.

"Sorry, mate, no bolts or nothing like that at all."

"Oh well. Thank you, very much. Here's your wrench."

"You poor guy. Good on you, mate, good on you."

I got back on my bike—on my tricycle—and began to wonder if I would be able to finish. I visualized cartilage shredding with each pedal stroke. It hurt more and more and I was going slower and slower.

The road is old and on the rough side. There were bumpy patches and that's really the only complaint you hear about that race because there's a constant stream of vibration.

My inept mechanic abilities surfaced again because my tribars were loose and rattled constantly on that bumpy road—it was really annoying me. My knees were screaming; now I had this sound to deal with. I wondered if it was time to pull over for good. There's nothing wrong with being exhausted, maybe throwing up a couple of times, but doing permanent damage to your knees?

The aid stations kept me going. "Good on you matey, good on you!" There were little kids and moms and dads and they served Gatorade and all the other things athletes crave. But the one thing I couldn't figure out was when they said, "Biscuit! Would you like a biscuit, mate?"

Biscuit? I thought of Shredded Wheat biscuits. Who would want a biscuit? Or was it a dog biscuit? Finally I took one, and it turned out to be a chocolate chip cookie, homemade. From then on, I yelled, "Biscuit? Biscuit?"

I pulled over once again at an aid station near mile seventy and managed to snag some medical tape. I wrapped my tri-bars as tightly as I could and got back on my trike. I was sure I looked like a Shriner, with one of those goofy little motorcycles, and I felt like a chimpanzee.

My knees were hurting more than ever, and my bars were still rattling. The tape didn't do any good, and then the tape—part of it broke off—unraveled and got stuck in my back wheel. So on top of the rattling, on top of the screaming knees, now I heard, "Fwip, fwip, fwip." I was sure I was in Hell. All I needed was someone to drip water drops on my head and shine a bright light in my eyes. It was no fun. I was one of the many triathletes inspired by the pain of Julie Moss crawling to the finish of her first ironman—but now it didn't seem to be a motivating factor for me.

Fwip, fwip, rattle, rattle, squeak, squeak. This was worse than my first triathlon.

The Julie Moss thing hit Iowa in 1982 and shortly thereafter I finished my first half ironman—the All Iowa Triathlon. It was an ironman distance and a half-ironman distance because back then there was no such thing as a short-distance triathlon. Oh sure, in San Diego they did, but Iowa—we had all seen the Ironman on television and thought, 'Oh, *that's* a triathlon.' I did the half ironman. Iowa, in July, is ninety percent humidity and above ninety degrees. It's not flat like Nebraska; it's actually rolling hills and torturous on a bike. There was one aid station at the halfway point of the ride. Three Cub Scouts and a den mother with a couple of bananas and some water. I rode my old Gitane that I bought when I was thirteen, and there I was riding it again at nineteen.

Fwip, fwip, rattle, rattle, squeak, squeak.

I was too lazy to get off my bike and take the tape out. I looked like a small, one-man band—those guys with a drum, a horn and a cymbal. I provided a little on-course entertainment for everybody.

Even though it was the Julie Moss finish that inspired me to enter a triathlon, I did that half ironman because my dad was a really good runner, one of the best Master's runners in Iowa, and the house was clogged with trophies. Here I was, nineteen years old and my dad could kick my butt. I had run track in high school, but never farther than eight hundred meters. Dad was doing marathons, so for me, it was one of those father-son things, like, "I'll outdo him by doing this half ironman." So that started it and now I was suffering away in Australia.

With about twenty to thirty miles to go, I pulled up to a bike crew van and took the freakin' tape out of my back wheel. I felt no need to rush. I waddled over and said, "Do you guys have a bolt for this?" I pointed at my low-rider seat. They did, it was my dream of dreams.

As much of a relief as it was, I didn't know if I would be able to run two steps, or need to find an orthopedic surgeon in the medical tent. "Excuse me," I'd say, once I was in the transition area. "I have some meniscus tears here. Yeah, forget the IV, I just need some arthroscopy."

Now, there's a weird thing that happens on this course. These wonderful kids near town, whom I've seen several times throughout the day, have their evil twins out at the end of the bike course. In town they're waving and cheering; they're the best. It's cool to have these little guys cheering for you, but then later in the race—maybe they're the same kids—they started asking for stuff. "Can I have your water bottle? Can I have your sunglasses?" I'm in such a foul mood at this point. "No, you can't have my sunglasses! Get away from me! You little thugs!"

I came upon one of these gangs, completely irritated. I ripped off my tri-bars and threw them to the kids. "Here you go," I said. I had taken care of the fwipping, the rattling, and my knees, so my mood vastly improved as I got into town.

The townspeople were wonderful. They were all over the place cheering like mad, and drinking, too. I got into transition and put on my racing flats. As I ran out, I passed the finish line area, figuring the winners were out having a steak dinner.

My knees felt okay. Finishing seemed like a possibility now. It was warm; it was still summer—the tail end of summer and the sun was still up—and hot. It was a two-loop run course with some pretty solid hills. Because I'm a relatively good runner and was way back in the field when I started, I passed a lot of people. It wasn't long before I began to feel bad and beat up and tired. My pain in a marathon always starts near the twenty-mile mark, and here I was at ten miles feeling that way. It might as well have been one hundred the way I felt. I witnessed so many unfolding dramas around me—someone clutching a cramp in their calf and wincing, somebody throwing up, somebody walking in raw misery, crying, others silent and completely focused.

Nobody talked. What happened on the run course was fascinating to see from the inside out. It was great for me to experience as an editor of *Triathlete* and as a fan of the sport—to be in there and actually *feel* the distress, too. It was a quiet, shared misery that connected everybody, and it connects the sport as a whole. It brings to the surface an interesting state of mind, an altered state of consciousness. At that point in an ultra-endurance event, senses are extraordinarily alive and emotional blocks get rooted out and burned. I've never experienced such a hallucinating state in a marathon. Wherever you are on the measuring stick of time in your life, whatever sorts of things are happening, you can easily revisit those memories during an ironman.

I got a glow stick at some point. I always kept at a jog but even as I got closer to the end, it seemed impossible in some ways—it felt like it was going to be a week before I finished.

Finally, I was about a quarter of a mile out of town and could hear this Aussie throng chanting. A chill went through me. I turned onto the main street and had to do an L-turn. I could see the klieg lighting—the sky was glowing. One hundred meters later I turned left and had the final two-hundred-meter stretch before me, fully carpeted with stands on either side, packed with people. The image transcended all my troubles. I had spent all day to get to that point. I slapped hands with people as I ran by and there was this woman, just drunk and singing and happy, telling me, "You're an ironman! You're an ironman!" It was thrilling and it made up for all the fwipping.

Crossing the finish line was more than I'd ever imagined even though I'd seen it so many times—ever since 1982. It was tremendous. The first time around, maybe you think from your training that, 'Yeah, I could do this,' but you don't know it. You don't know it in your bones until you actually cross the finish line and when you do cross the finish line it's a life-altering experience because of the way you feel about yourself or see yourself, you know there's something you can do that you couldn't do before. You can feel something turn in a deep, deep way. Athletics may not be the most important thing in life, but it can have a huge impact.

I'll tell you, I've seen a lot of finish lines at a lot of races, but to me, I've never seen a finish like the one in Australia. Maybe that's because I was in the race. I'm sure that affects my opinion. Afterward, pro triathlete Greg Welch, who is such a great guy in this sport, came up to me—just beaming—and said, "Good on you, mate!" He knew I was editor of *Triathlete*, but now he knew I could really write about this sport. I mean, he always respected me as a person and was very kind to me, but now I had gained a new measure of respect in his eyes. I wasn't on the sidelines anymore. I was one of them.

T. J. returned to Ironman Australia in 1999 and avoided any fwipping, mastering the course in 11:59:13. In 2000 T. J. left Triathlete *magazine to become a writer and editor in New York City. But he didn't leave triathlon—he trained for and finished the Hawaii Ironman that year.*

WORLD'S HARDEST VACATION

KEITH PEEK

DATE OF BIRTH: SEPTEMBER 23, 1959

RACE: IRONMAN LANZAROTE 2000

TIME: 13:04:27

By 3 A.M. I had four hours of disturbed sleep. That would be it, a very long day was beckoning. Anne awoke and soon coffee with strawberry jam croissants were hurriedly being consumed. I packed and checked that everything I needed was in my warm-up bag. Then kisses, good luck, and good-bye from Anne before I left to catch the bus.

It was dark and I couldn't see my new friend and fellow first-timer Dave. We had met on the plane to Lanzarote and stayed at the same resort, Club La Santa. We had arranged to meet that morning, not so much out of necessity, but more for the mutual comfort of seeing a familiar face before facing unfamiliar territory. I boarded the coach alone and sat down. Some people laughed and joked nervously; many were silent as we took the thirty-minute journey to Puerto del Carmen. We were the first competitors to arrive and quickly went through the security procedure before entering the transition. I rushed to my bike bag on the beach and deposited my two-litre Camelbak fresh from the fridge. Next I filled the aerobottle and pumped the tyres. Bar wet suit, I was ready with two hours to go. I took advantage of the empty loos and then sauntered around transition admiring the bikes and wacky items people strap to them. I found Dave trying to convince himself that a loo stop was required even though his body was not responding.

Transition filled rapidly and the queue for the loos got longer. With forty-five minutes to go, I changed into my wet suit and deposited my warm-up bag with the marshals. Anne, my children Ben and Holly, and Dave's wife, Kerry, arrived. We chatted and joked and Kerry asked Dave for an impromptu camcorder interview as he tried to convince his body yet again for a second loo stop. With twenty minutes to go, the call for competitors went out. Dave was still in the loo queue and I said my good-byes. First cock-up when Anne asked me if I intended to swim in my shoes and socks.

On the beach the PA was in full swing, and a large crowd gathered as the sun began to rise. The atmosphere was tense and electric. I was in the front row, wide on the right. The pros were ahead by twenty yards. And the mayhem began.

Although I was in the front row I had to cut across left to the first buoy and soon became part of the washing machine melee. Ten minutes later, clear of the fist drills, I settled into a rhythm. I took many people in the swim and frequently got boxed in on the marker buoy line. But hey, it was easy; the water temperature was perfect and the sea clear as I watched the sunrise above and fishes below to pass time. Soon, I completed the first lap and walked up the beach, around the marker, and checked my split. Thirty minutes. Better than I'd expected and I felt okay. Back in for a second lap and although it was easier to find clear water, I again got boxed in against the marker buoy line. The sun was up and I was bored watching fish so it was time for elbows and arms as I put on a spurt and fought to pass several slower swimmers. I approached the beach having completed the swim in just a shade over one hour. To say I was pleased was an understatement.

I walked up the beach into the showers, removed the wet suit, picked up my bike bag, and went into the change tent. There was kit flying everywhere, nudity permitted, and no time to blush. Off with the swim kit, on with the bike kit, don Camelbak, smear with sunscreen, and jog to the bike. Bike bottle off, heart-rate monitor on, bottle on, wave to Anne and the kids, and I was off after a nine-minute transition.

I quickly got into a rhythm on the bike and started drinking every few minutes. Then I peered at the heart-rate monitor and it was 162 beats-per-minute. Panic set in, as I did not plan to go above 150. It felt easy though and I was cruising at over twenty miles per hour. I convinced myself that the cause was adrenaline. I kept checking and it slowly came down over the next hour to settle at about 140.

I ignored the first feed station, but ate on cue every fifteen minutes. Soon I was heading down to El Golfo, a village on the southwest side of the island, cruising on the aerobars at over thirty miles per hour.

I saw the first technical failure on the side of the road in El Golfo. For a split second I wanted to help, before turning my attention to the hills. An American pro, Joel Hennings, whom I had met by the pool, passed me easily. But his day turned sour later, to finish in over thirteen hours. After El Golfo the serious climbs started and large numbers of good cyclists began to pass me.

I was spinning up the hills in the Fire Mountains as more out-of-the-saddle riders passed me. I kept my spirits high and resisted the temptation to go with the flow by muttering, "crap swimmer" to everyone who passed me.

The Fire Mountains' roads are rough climbs that are short

and steep, but it wasn't long before I was back on the aerobars heading down to Club La Santa. Then it was up then down to Famara, before starting the long climb to Teguise and the high mountains in the north. I passed the 90K marker after Teguise and checked my split, three hours and eight minutes.

The climbs were longer with steeper sections in the north, but I continued to spin, eat, and drink plenty of water (testament to my three loo stops) as more 'crap swimmers' passed me. At the top of Mirador de Haria, I stopped for my special feed bag. I took the sports drink, energy bars, some chewing gum and dumped the rest. The steep technical descent from there made it an enjoyable ride as I passed several nervous descenders.

Soon I was climbing again. The view on approach to Mirador del Rio was awesome as I peered out over the island of Graciosa. I was out of the saddle and over the top with the knowledge that all the hard climbs were behind me. The descent to the village of Orzola was fast and winding. In the final ten minutes it was like riding on a washboard, which made it tiring on my hands. From there it was south along the coast, on a rolling road with a light wind in my face. Next I cut back inland and there was more climbing. I continued through St. Bartolome and Tias resting on the aerobars during the descents. In the final 10K Dave passed me, probably in a rush to get to the loo!

The party atmosphere in Puerto del Carmen carried me swiftly into transition. I dismounted and a marshal quickly took my bike. I had to stop him in order to retrieve my heart-rate monitor. I was off to transition for a full kit change and more sunscreen.

I was into my stride quickly although I felt a slight pain in my left foot. Encouragement from the family and crowd helped me cover the first lap in a little over an hour. During the second lap the pain in the foot got worse and I began to slow down.

Later I would learn it was a stress fracture that held me back. I walked every aid station and took only water. The third lap was tough but I ignored the pain and focused on each aid station and began to consume Power Gels. At that point I knew I had the run mentally in the bag. I collected my final green-coloured cord and I started the last lap.

I drank Coke at every aid station and this seemed to spur me on and increase my stride whilst overtaking several runners.

The last two hundred yards and everyone was shouting, but I heard only Anne, Ben, and Holly. I passed another competitor and Holly joined me on the run. With the crowd cheering I put on what I thought was a sprint but I couldn't keep up with Holly. With a few yards to go I shouted to her to slow down and we crossed the line together in 13:04:27.

I had a brief head-in-hands-watery-eye moment before shaking hands with the race director and moving on for the next athlete to take their bow.

The medical tent was like a war zone, something like a scene from *M.A.S.H.* I walked for quite a while before finding an empty bed to sit on. A medic asked if I was okay. "Do you need an IV drip?"

"No, I'm fine," was my initial response. Moments later, another medic asked the same question. This time I said I felt a slight cramp in the 'sprint' to the line.

"You should have a drip," he said.

"Oh what the hell, okay."

Several ironmen had recommended it to me as the best way for a rapid recovery. I lay on the bed hooked up to the IV line and looked around. The guy next to me was shivering vigorously. The bed opposite had someone asleep, or at least I hoped. The ambulance siren screamed and an asthmatic was carried off on bottled oxygen. I was still smiling though. I felt good. As the saline drip replenished my body, I reflected on what I had just done with my family beside me. Several more watery-eye moments passed before I was unhooked and off for a massage. After the massage I collected my medal and T-shirt and had the official photo taken. It was on a stage, which required a step up; not the easiest step I've ever made.

I met up with Dave and the conversation quickly turned to the race. Soon we were talking a good ironman race in which we shave hours off our times.

Keith Peek is a Ph.D. biochemist working in research and development in the United Kingdom. He was inspired to become an ironman after watching the 1996 Ironman Lanzarote during a family holiday to the Canary Islands.

THE BEST OF TIMES

J. P. REED

DATE OF BIRTH: NOVEMBER 20, 1956

RACE: IRONMAN EUROPE 1990

TIME: 10:39:39

I traveled to Roth, West Germany, to compete in Ironman Europe. I say West Germany, because even though the wall had come down there was still a lot of animosity. The West Germans considered it an invasion really. They were not happy about East Germans coming into *their* country. Germans didn't recognize it as one country yet. There was a lot of pain and it was evident to us American tourists who didn't even speak the language.

There were only sixty-four Americans in the race. Fortunately my friend Jim was one of them and his wife, Hilde, was our translator. Although the signs were well marked with stick-figure swimmers, bikers, and runners, the meetings left us anxious. After speaking for twenty minutes in German, race officials provided a three-minute synopsis in a variety of languages, including English. We always wondered, 'What are we missing here?'

I knew a few words: *wasser*, or 'water.' And *cola*. But I never knew what I was going to get. The international word for 'beer' is *beer*. And the beer was fantastic.

We had been there a week already, sampling the bountiful homebrews of the local pubs. Adolph, the twenty-something son of our B&B owners, went along on almost every excursion as our tour guide. The week leading up to the race allowed me to adjust to the time change and get acclimated to the weather. Those first few days were rainy and cool. I live in Houston. I don't do well in the cold. And I was racing there in hopes of gaining one of the forty coveted slots available in my age group for the Hawaii Ironman.

The transition bags and my bike had to be dropped off the afternoon before the race. I was so keyed up and nervous that it took about four hours to get my bike and bags packed just so. After dropping the bike and bags off, my wife, Dianne, and I went to the "Noodle Party." The food was really good and plentiful: pasta and sauce (both creamy and tomato), salad with dressing, desserts (yes, more than one!), and yogurt. To drink, there was water of all types and non-alcoholic beer.

It turned out to be a gorgeous day for the race. We got up really early so we could park on the far side of the course from our Gusthoff at the swim start. This enabled Dianne to drive from the swim course to where the run would start and finish, which was about a 10K distance. At the race site the police let us park near an exit so Dianne could get out after the start of the race. We walked down, aired up my tires, checked all my gear again for the fifteenth time, and then sat around nervously anticipating the start. Anyone who needed to use the bathroom before the race—and who doesn't?—was pointed in the direction of the woods. Men were pointed in one direction, women in another.

The swim start was done in two waves of seven hundred and six hundred fifty because of the canal's tight quarters. The nice thing about swimming in a canal is that it's hard to get off course. I was in the second wave because of my estimated finish time. The gun fired for the first wave, and bedlam ensued. Those of us in wave number two started inching into the seventy-one-degree water. Actually, it was fairly comfortable in my wet suit, booties, and neoprene hood. The second gun fired, and we were off. The first two hundred meters were pretty crazy, but then I settled in behind a swimmer in a pastel swimsuit (no wet suit). He was easy to see in the clear water. I drafted off him almost all the way to the turnaround and then lost him in the crowd as we rounded the buoys. On the way back I was on my own for about half the distance, so I sighted off the towers at the lock where we would finish the swim. About halfway back I looked to my right and there was my buddy in the pastel swimsuit, so I tucked in for a ride to the ramp. The swim was over incredibly fast, as I finished in 1:08:32.

The whole incline out of the water, up to the levee, was the changing tent. The top of the levee was used for the run and the other side of the slope was for the bikes. The changing tent was coed. But shucks, all the women competitors were put in the first wave to ease the calculations of their times at the finish, and they were all gone except for a few really slow swimmers. There were, however, a few female change attendants.

It was important to do all of our changing in the tent. The only thing we could put on at our bicycle was our helmet and shoes. The transition area was so tight, officials wanted us in and out fast. A German pro got disqualified for not following this rule.

After changing, I needed to get to my bike, which was over the hill about one hundred feet, and walk it out of the transition area at the top of the hill about three hundred yards away. My transition took eight minutes and seven seconds.

The bike course was three loops. People were everywhere.

Every time I came to a village, a sharp turn, or a climb, the crowds got larger. The numbers were really heavy on the climbs. The people helped me up the hills by shouting "hup" or blowing whistles in rhythm to my pedal stroke. As I rode through the villages, the locals had tables and chairs lined along the streets and they toasted me with their beer as I flew by. In fact they toasted and drank every time a biker rode by, and they were sloshed by the third loop. The ride could have been a lot tougher without those cheering crowds to help me up the climbs.

About 8K from the end of the bike, I downshifted to an easier gear to get my legs loosened up for the marathon ahead. The 26.2-miler was the part I doubted most. At this point it was too late to turn back. I completed the bike segment in 5:27:08. As I rode into the transition area, I spotted Dianne in the crowd and gave her a big smile because she knew as well as I did that my day had gone really well up to this point. I dismounted, and my bike was immediately taken from me by an attendant. I passed the hundreds of transition bags, found mine, and headed for the changing tent. And what do you know, I caught a few of the women on that bike ride! I finished taking in the sights and finally changed. Out of the tent, I began to run. Then I began to walk. I decided it would be in my best interest to drink a can of nutritional beverage and the water bottle full of Exceed that I had in my changing bag.

With the fluid down, I changed gears to run. I was already anticipating the first aid station. I got to walk there, it was all part of the plan. Finally it appeared in the distance, only one hundred yards ahead. My eager anticipation amounted to only a thirty-second walk, but the aid stations kept appearing in front of me, and those thirty-second breaks were nonetheless appreciated as I rumbled along.

The run course was fairly easy. It was primarily on the levee, along the canal that we swam in. No real hills to speak of, nothing more difficult than running up the hills in Memorial Park in Houston.

At 8K I met Ian, a fellow Houstonian coming back from the first turnaround, which was at 15K. He was flying and Jan Wanklyn (the eventual women's winner) was about twenty feet ahead of him. Just after meeting Ian and Jan, I ran through the village of Haimpfarrich, and I saw the backside of Amy, another familiar Texan. But before I could catch her and say anything, she pulled away from me. Here I began to play mind games with myself to figure out which Texas competitor I'd meet next. First I saw Joe from Austin, then I recognized Denis from Houston. I met Amy again about one hundred yards before the 15K turnaround.

At the turnaround I picked up my special-foods bag (a water bottle of Exceed and a peanut butter and strawberry jelly sandwich). I ate about half the sandwich. That's all my stomach would take. I inhaled the Exceed. The aid stations kept flying by. At 30K I looked at my watch and realized I had an hour and a half to cover the last 12K to break eleven hours. My emotions were hard to control. I started to cry, then yelled at myself to bring back my wits. I felt like I was flying that last 12K. I passed people about one per minute. Earlier in the run it was probably one person every three or four minutes. And yet I calculated later that my pace on the last 12K was 9:41 per mile.

About half a mile from the finish I saw Joe. He had come back out after finishing in 10:12 to cheer me on in my first ironman. He yelled at me, "Now you can say you're an ironman!" My pace quickened. I was so tired but it was mixed with excitement and anxiety. I finished strongly, passing two more people before the finish line. My emotions were intense. I completed the marathon in 3:52:30 and the race overall in

10:39:39. Unfortunately I didn't qualify to compete in Hawaii. In fact, I didn't even come close. As the slots were passed down to those who wanted to go to Hawaii, the last person to accept finished in 10:12:55.

J. P. Reed has been competing in triathlons since 1984. He has since raced in six other ironman races and qualified for Hawaii at Ironman Canada 1992. His first ironman, however, remains his fastest.

A LONG WORKOUT DAY

MARA BARTH

DATE OF BIRTH: MARCH 20, 1970

RACE: IRONMAN AUSTRIA 2000

TIME: 12:51:45

In 1999 Mara Barth began working as a travel consultant in Chicago, making arrangements for triathletes to go to races all over the world. She decided to see for herself why people were going to the ends of the earth for ironman.

After forty-two marathons 26.2 miles was getting to be old hat. Not that I'm bored with the marathon, it's the perfect distance for me. I was just getting a bit cocky because I felt like I'd always be able to finish, even if I had to walk.

Ironman was a race I wasn't completely sure I'd finish. My goal was fifteen hours, but I would have been perfectly happy with anything under the seventeen-hour limit. My mantra was, 'This is just a long workout day.'

I didn't start with the other competitors when the gun went off. There was a bottleneck getting onto the beach, but because of my tardy arrival I managed to avoid the pounding at the start. I took a minute to wade in and set my goggles just so before diving in, then immediately started to panic. *What the hell am I doing here? I'm out of my mind. Look at these people, they all know exactly what they're doing and I don't have a clue.* There was splashing everywhere and I couldn't get a breathing pattern and had to take choppy strokes to keep from swimming over people. I spotted a dock on my right and wondered if I could somehow swim under the dock and hang there until everyone forgot about me. Then I could lurk off into the bushes until tomorrow.

Then I remembered: I'm a swimmer! Not as fast as a law-abiding bullet, but I know how to breathe, for God's sake! In my unconscious quest for the dock, I now was far to the right of the crowd and started taking breaths only to the right. This way I saw only the crowd on the dock and not the splashfest to my left. By the time I was at the edge of the dock I was fine. I saw Mike—my nineteen-year-old, future ironman brother—cheering for me. I tried to wave as I stroked by, hamming it up for the cameras.

I got into a good groove, long steady strokes, rotating the hips, extra stretch at the end. Trying to be strong and as efficient as possible, with very little kicking in the interest of having fresh legs for the bike. I was passing people and could barely see the buoys, but was still at the fringe of the crowd and not too concerned until the turnaround buoy, when I had to swim across the crowd to turn. I knew I wasn't swimming the most efficient line, but stresswise this was the path of least resistance.

We were to swim the last eight hundred meters in a canal to the transition. I could sense the shore approaching but couldn't sight the canal. I put faith in the swimmers ahead of me and kept my head down. As we made our way into the canal so did the water flow, and we got caught in the draft of those in front of us. It made for a nice speedy finish. I felt my hands brush the ramp, stood up, and saw I was out at 1:01:40.

Transition was fun, except trying to wrestle a sports bra over a wet body. The bike is my least favorite by far. I gave Humphrey (the mini Beanie Baby camel I had pinned on the top tube of my bike for good luck) a little kiss and took off.

The bike course starts off with about 25K of gentle rolling hills along the lakeshore—breathtaking scenery with chalets and towns along the way. Each town was having its own beerfest for the spectators. The next 20K was home to the hill from hell and its bastard cousin. After that it was an easy coast back to the start of the loop, which we did three times.

As expected, I got passed by everyone I beat out of the water. I was prepared for this so I didn't panic and held my pace and concentrated on drinking. I inhaled half of a PB&J during the first hour as well.

I had been over the course earlier so I knew what was coming. When you think you're at the top, you're not! I developed a method of counting the pedal strokes once I was out of the saddle. *Just look down and count.* It was too depressing to look up and see how much farther it was to the top. The first time over I gave Humphrey a little pat. *Only two more of those to go, buddy, and we're home free.*

All the spectators were shouting, "Hup, hup, hup . . . Supa! . . . Bravo!" They were armed with a variety of noisemakers and the start list so they could read our numbers and shout names.

Just as I started to enjoy the great speed on the downside, I realized I had a flat. Steering into the grass, I hopped off the bike prepared for my usual ten-minute tire change. Fortunately for me, two spectators guided and helped me through it in less than five. I coasted back into town, finishing the first loop as I snacked on PB&J and bananas.

I came through the crowd, saw my brother taking pictures, and barked an order for another tube to my iron crew. My husband, Jeff, is great support and my most generous sponsor. Deepak and Kirti, my boss and his wife, were there as well. They likely would be anyway because Deepak runs a company that provides race- and travel-related services to multisport athletes. Deepak is usually traveling as a host with various groups to ironman races. He's the ideal boss for a triathlete. He was very supportive of my training. (Translation: Less time at work.)

The second loop I continued to get passed but at least I didn't have a flat. I had been grabbing bananas at all the aid stations and was, at this point, on the fourth one. I figured it was the best defense to keep from cramping. Those two hills got tougher the second time around and in the midst of them, I got lapped by eventual winner Jürgen Zäck like I was a statue. Still, I refused to get swept into a panic and tried to speed it up, knowing I had one more loop before the run. My hope was to get through the bike with enough time to walk the marathon if I needed to, and my pace was allowing for that.

I saw Jeff, Mike, Kirti, and Deepak as I came around for the third loop, a bike tube dangling within my reach. Peace of mind is a beautiful thing, and having two spares was a comfort for me. I headed out for the third time and—wait a second—did I say "gentle rolling hills"? I tried to stay in my saddle and spin as much as possible, but it was a slow spin and I heard Joe, a client and fellow competitor, approach me. In his heavy southern drawl (with the bark of a drill sergeant) he said, "Move your ass!" I didn't have the energy for a witty response as he flew by.

Back to the hills. By now I knew it takes about two hundred pedal strokes to get to the top of the first hill, a few more for the second. I was going so slow I imagined birds would start nesting in my helmet. It might have been quicker to get off and walk the bike. As I neared the top a young Austrian fellow reached for the back of my bike in an offer to push me the rest of the way. I'm sure I scared the daylights out of him with my shout of "No!" I didn't want to finish the race knowing I had someone push me the last ten feet of that Rupertiberg (the name of the bastard cousin hill). Poor thing, he only wanted to help.

Finally I crested the top and enjoyed going downhill again. I almost started to cry at this point because I realized I had a good chance to finish, but for the sake of the last 25K I held it together. I took it easy this last segment, coasting every chance I got and conserving energy for the run. I entered into the transition and happily passed my bike off to a volunteer. My butt was sore but my spirits were soaring. *I have almost nine hours to do the marathon.*

As soon as I put on my running shoes, my feet and legs felt like they were shouting with joy. 'Yes! We know this part! This is our gig!' From this point forth they could go on autopilot. Getting to the marathon was like being with an old friend again. I couldn't believe how great I felt and I smiled easily for the camera and everyone I saw.

The run course is out-and-back in one direction, then out-and-back in another direction (this second part coming dangerously close to our hotel). We do this twice. With the way the course is set up, I got to see a lot of our group and we encouraged each other along the way.

My plan was to push the first 21K, walking only the water stops. I would check in with myself from there for guidelines on how to continue. I tried to take one of my Power Gels at the first stop, but what works for me in a regular marathon didn't work there and I almost gagged. At the next water stop I grabbed a Coke and man, did that taste good! Wow—elixir of the gods!

The aid stations were only 2K apart and after stopping at each one I was getting a rest break about every twelve minutes. As I approached the 8K mark, I saw Joe walking ahead. Payback time. "Move your ass!" I yelled as I came upon him.

"I knew that would come back to haunt me," he said.

I was tempted to stay and walk with him, but I felt too good to slow down. I passed Roger, another one of our clients and ironman veteran, near 12K.

"You're smokin'!" he said, and with that I picked up the pace.

Jeff and Mike were at the turnaround in town and I was still smiling. The run course is flat and shady. The spectators at the cafés along the course were entertaining. I imagine some of them were there for the long haul, the drunken rowdiness being my only clue. It was easy to get them shouting with just a quick wave.

I arrived at the 21K mark and judged my condition. Still not ready to walk, I devised Plan B: Run to 32K and then walk the last 10K. It began to rain, which was no problem for me because I was soaked anyway. At the 32K mark I was ready to follow up with my plan and walk, but vanity appeared when I least expected it. The ESPN camera (a two-man crew on a motorcycle) had tracked me down and started leading me along. *Damn, can't walk now—this is television.* They stayed with me for about ten minutes and by then I felt good again and figured I'd take it another kilometer before walking. No such chance—the camera showed up again, and stayed for another kilometer. I was psyched to be filmed but had really wanted to walk. Finally they took off, giving me a thumbs-up as I continued into town.

For the last 5K I finally gave myself a chance to walk. I ran the first five minutes of each kilometer and walked the rest. It worked well, and I was getting through them in about seven minutes.

As I ran over the last ramp (the perfectly flat run course had been marred with a couple of man-made ramps, a mean trick, I'd say), I was pulling arm over arm on the banister to get up.

"There she is!" It was Deepak, announcing my arrival.

I was within a kilometer of the finish and needed only to round the bleachers and come back in. I couldn't believe I had broken thirteen hours, with a marathon time of 4:36, which is about what I do in a marathon anyway.

I high-fived the crowd and leaped across the finish into Jeff's arms. I collected my medal and a giant Austrian gingerbread cookie. It was such a great high to finish. I knew of only one way to re-create it—do another ironman. As much of a pain as training was at times, it was rewarded in that moment of personal glory. It was like I had heard a coach say: Ironman training was like working for ten months without a paycheck. But finishing was priceless.

TWICE UPON A FULL MOON

DAKIN FERRIS

DATE OF BIRTH: JULY 30, 1960

RACE: IRONMAN CANADA 1999

TIME: 15:39:52

Dakin Ferris, an attorney living in San Francisco, completed an iron-man to raise money for the Leukemia and Lymphoma Society of America and grieve the loss of a love.

I had dreamed of this day for a long time. As I looked around at my fellow competitors, I felt a special respect for them. Each of us was committed to the premise that whatever fate threw in our path that day, neither pain nor brain would stop our progress until we crossed the finish line. I have always drawn tremendous comfort when others shared my delusions. With 140.6 miles of terrain to cover before midnight, this was no exception.

Next to me were five friends from the 'Ironteam,' a special team we formed to extend the reach of the Leukemia Society's Team-in-Training program, as well as to test our own physical limits. There were eighteen others on our team, but they were lost somewhere in the sea of wet suits. We had been training together for almost twenty months, and as I waded in Okanagan Lake before the start, I felt proud that in the process of getting here, we had raised almost two hundred thousand dollars for leukemia and lymphoma research and treatment.

I was motivated by personal loss, and as I stood there, I thought about my first visit with Pam in her hospital room. She was surrounded by tubes and things that dripped and beeped and lights that changed colors. There was a sense of serenity on her face that belied the trauma that hours of surgery had witnessed upon her body.

From her hospital window I could see the full moon shining on the Marin County hills. When I saw the hills the next day, I noticed people running, walking, and biking on a path that followed a sleepy marsh stream. Someday, I thought, we would go for a walk along that stream.

Instead, I found myself toeing the line of an ironman triathlon. In the final minutes before the start, my anxiety rose significantly. *I sure wish Pam were with me today.*

Boom! There was a surreal quality when the cannon blast signaled the start of the race—as if everything was in slow motion. Against the advice of ironman veterans, I decided to start right in the middle of it all, waist deep in the chilly water, with nearly 1800 other competitors surrounding me. Personal safety suggested that I start at the back or to the side, but I wanted to be right in the middle of it, and that's where I stood. It was 7 A.M. *I am glad I'm here with my team. I can't imagine doing this alone.*

As I took my first strokes, I thought about how I love the swim portion of triathlon. Maybe it's the excitement of the start, or the variables of feet, elbows, and being directionally challenged, but whatever; it's just my favorite. This wasn't the case for some of my teammates, though. Many of them later recounted how they were kicked, elbowed, punched, and swam over. One even lost his goggles.

I never experienced any of this. I was protected during my

swim by a cocoon, suggested to me the night before in a guided meditation conducted for our team. It may sound hokey, but it worked like a charm. As suggested, the cocoon came to me upon my first collision, and it protected me the rest of the way. When I felt someone's presence, I simply swam around them or provided extra space. I interpreted all incursions as benign, and swam my race, at my pace, in relative peace and harmony.

Before long I rounded the last buoy and headed for shore. On this final leg, I found myself staring at the moon setting over the hills and thought about the thunderstorm to which I awoke that morning. I feared most a repeat of the 104-degree inferno many of these competitors experienced the year before.

A few more strokes, a wave to a scuba diver watching from the bottom, and I was done with the swim. At 1:06:42 I was right on schedule. I ran from the water to the two most attractive volunteers I could find. I lay down and let them strip off my wet suit. I chuckled to myself thinking about how one of my teammates had joked about going "commando" under his wet suit and giving everyone a little surprise.

The first 40 miles of the 112-mile bike course were almost as fun as the swim. No hard hills, and the air was still cool. *Hey everyone, look at me! I am doing the Man!* Despite all I had learned in the previous year about pacing, I pushed much harder than I should have. Part of me simply wanted to cover as much ground as I could before many of my teammates would start to pass me— an ego play, pure and simple—but onward I pressed. I was too darn excited to do anything else!

In shorter races, you can make this sort of mistake and still finish strongly. Ironman veterans will be quick to tell you, however, that whether it's ego, excitement, or poor judgment, each can take you out of an ironman in less than a heartbeat. I was no exception. As I began the six-mile climb up Richter Pass, I started to bonk. *Okay, don't panic. If you want to finish this thing, slow down—way down—and start eating and drinking.*

It never got much better from that point forward. I pedaled onward, but by midday the clouds had cleared, the sun was beating down, and serious fatigue was setting in. At mile eighty I was too woozy to eat or drink almost anything. I knew this meant I was way over the line. For the first time, a little doubt crept into my mind.

The last fifteen miles of the bike course were grueling. The heat, dehydration, and exhaustion continued to take their toll, and after six hours in the saddle my butt ached. The prospect of being allowed to start running a marathon was all I wanted. *I have to get off this bike.*

Finally I rode into town past the wonderful townsfolk who had been out there cheering all day. My cycling time was 6:57:23, seven minutes off my fastest ever for this distance. I handed someone my bike, grabbed my transition bag, and headed off to change into my running gear. In the transition tent, I fought the impulse to get sick, and after sitting for a few minutes, forced myself to down some flat Pepsi and pretzels.

Twenty minutes and three refills later, I was not feeling any better. It was gut-check time. Intuitively, I knew this was my window. *If I don't keep moving, I'll be down for the count.* I decided to keep moving. My revised plan: Start walking and don't run until you feel like it. *With eight and a half hours to go before they shut the race down, I should have plenty of time to finish.*

A few teammates passed me a couple of hundred yards into my final 26.2 miles of this odyssey. I would have given anything to be able to run with them, as my misery was looking for a little company, but it just wasn't in me. I walked. After about a mile I saw the lead male coming at me. I fantasized about turning around and following him in while waving to the cheering crowd. I took my humor as a sign that I was feeling better and commenced a light jog. *I know I can do this thing. Just keep at it.*

I think I had about six or seven miles of the run behind me before it all started to fall apart in earnest. The covering on my left running insert came off, and before long it was digging mercilessly into my heel. I started walking again. By mile thirteen, I was convinced that the Grand Canyon had opened an annex in my left heel. I took the inserts out and walked on the uncushioned soles. *I think I am going to be sick.*

At mile nineteen, I was limping badly. My body ached everywhere and waves of nausea came and went. Looking at my watch, I was disappointed my body wasn't living up to the Grand Finale I had written for this race months earlier. I considered firing the writer for a moment, but decided I could deal with him later.

Sometime around 8 P.M. the sun set, and for the first time that week the wind picked up and started blowing with gusto— straight at me. This was unexpected, and I was totally underdressed for it. I started shivering. *Okay, fine, whatever, keep bringing it on Lord because I am not stopping.*

And so it was. At 10:39:52 P.M. I crossed the finish line. To tell the truth, it was not the exultant finish or peak experience I expected. It felt more akin to being beaten and left for dead, but somehow having survived, and not knowing if it was for better or for worse. My friend Terry met me at the finish, I put my arm around her, and she guided me in my disoriented state to get my medal, a finisher's picture, a quick massage, and finally, mercifully, to my hotel.

Back at the hotel I managed to eat some real food, take a wonderfully delicious, warm bath, and, at three minutes to midnight, I turned on the TV and crawled into bed. The race was still showing live on local cable. *Cool! I can watch the last three minutes of the race and the fireworks that signal the end, and then rest these weary bones.* Of course, three minutes was two minutes and fifty-five seconds longer than my body had any intention of staying awake. My day was over. I was an ironman. Pam would have been proud.

What moves me most about my ironman experience is not that I crossed the finish line, but the forces that inspired me to undertake that goal, and everything that happened in the process of getting there. I learned a lot about myself. I believe we can take almost any experience in life and examine it as a microcosm of how we live the rest of our lives. For me, the more intense the experience, the more both my good qualities and my shadow side are revealed, side by side, obvious and undeniable. It is the self-knowledge that comes from this revelation that I think is some of the ripest fruit of the journey.

This particular journey started almost three years earlier as a result of my friend's cancer and subsequent passing. Watching her spirited, joyful life taken from her, I relearned something we all know intuitively but so easily forget as we get tied down in the minutiae of day-to-day living: Life is too short and precious not to devote energy to chase your dreams.

This dream would never have taken form without the Leukemia and Lymphoma Society of America's Team-in-Training program and the special group of people who for almost two years dedicated themselves to making this happen. I will forever be proud of having been associated with such an incredible group of people. We blazed new ground for Team-in-Training and, in the process, became a family.

Four weeks after my ironman finish, I got a message from a friend with whom I did Ironman Canada. He needed a last-minute replacement for a team that was doing a two-hundred-mile running relay from Calistoga to Santa Cruz that weekend. I signed on, even though it meant getting little sleep Saturday night. This is one of the great local races that I had wanted to do for some time.

My new teammates picked me up at 6:30 A.M., two days later. The first thing I noticed was our team name painted all over the van: THE VILLAGE IDIOTS. I knew immediately I was going to like these guys.

One of the Idiots asked me to run in the fifth slot, and so my first run as a newly minted Idiot was midafternoon. It felt reasonably solid at about an eight-minute-per-mile pace, especially in the hot Sonoma Valley sun. I handed off the baton, reclaimed my spot in the van, and estimated when I would be up again.

Shortly after midnight I started my second five-mile leg. The evening was enchanting by Bay Area standards: a full moon, warm weather, clear skies, and I was gliding along solitary, off-road paths with sections through neighborhoods unknown.

Two miles into this second run, my stride felt effortless. This was unusual for me. Running never feels effortless. At a 7:25 pace, however, this was easily my best run in years. Not like the shivering, limping walk I did for the last three hours in Canada. This was a magical groove.

And then, in a blinding flash, it hit me like a bolt of lightning. My heart raced and tears flooded my eyes. I staggered and nearly fell. *This is the path I saw from her room. This is the marsh.* While my teammates and I had dedicated Ironman Canada to the memory of a little girl named Emily Jordan, I realized in that moment every race I had run in the last three years had been for Pam. Long ago I gave up on my dream of walking along this path with her, *but she is here with me right now.*

KARA DOUGLASS THOM

Close your eyes.

The water laps your toes and envelops your skin. Close your eyes. The masses become silent and your heartbeat thunders. You have planned for today, talked about today, trained for today, imagined today, dreamed today, and yet you still don't know what to expect.

A cannon blows and you remember, as you dread the uncertainty and the harsh duration to come, to savor every second because in your memory it will be over in the minutes it takes to recount or reread from your journal.

Move, breathe, drink, eat. Move, breathe, drink, eat. Move and move. One hundred forty and six-tenths miles. Know tenderly, intimately every fiber of your being that propels you forward only because your brain says, 'Don't stop.' And don't stop. Move, breathe, drink, eat.

Manage your day. Stick to your plan. Be flexible. Just finish. Float when your mind and body detach and watch your body move without you—pushed by the crowd, the volunteers, who lust for your finish as if it were their own.

But it hurts. And you don't know for sure why you're doing this and what it will mean when you do. And then you see it. A banner, a clock, a frenzy of applause. And you know you made it happen through whatever means and power source you draw strength from.

Ironman will trivialize past hardship and prepare you to minimize those to come. It makes dreams come true. You have what it takes to bridge aspirations into accomplishments. Crossing that line embraces self: confidence, sacrifice, reliance, invention, worth. Finishing makes you your own hero.

It is my hope these stories have inspired those who rarely, if ever, see their heart rate go to max levels, provided encouragement to ironman athletes yet to be, and entertained anyone who has ever crossed an ironman finish line.

More books from Breakaway:

THE RUNNER'S LITERARY COMPANION: Great Stories and Poems about Running. 336 pages, hardcover, $23. ISBN: 1-55821-335-X "A literary treasure trove." —USA *Today*

THE RUNNER AND THE PATH: An Athlete's Quest for Meaning in Postmodern Corporate America. 272 pages, hardcover, $22. ISBN: 1-891369-28-8. A brilliant philosophical inquiry into balancing love, life, work, family, and running. It will open your eyes.

HOW RUNNING CHANGED MY LIFE: True Stories of the Power of Running. 208 pages, paperback, $15. ISBN: 1-891369-30-X. Stories to ignite the runner's soul.

THE QUOTABLE RUNNER: Great Moments of Wisdom, Inspiration, Wrongheadedness and Humor. Edited by Mark Will-Weber. Brief quotes and anecdotes from the greats of the sport. 304 pages. Hardcover, $22, ISBN: 1-55821-420-8 . Paperback, $13, ISBN: 1-891369-26-1. "Keep this book close to you at all times. It can't help but improve your spirits and your running." —*Runner's World.*

THE ELEMENTS OF EFFORT: Reflections on the Art and Science of Running. By John Jerome. 240 pages, $20, hardcover. ISBN: 1-55821-614-6 Lucid, philosophical short essays. "Shows runners the deep structure of their passion." —*Runner's World*

FIRST MARATHONS: Personal Encounters with the 26.2-Mile Monster. Edited by Gail Kislevitz. 304 pages, $23, hardcover. ISBN: 1-55821-673-1. Paperback, $15.00. ISBN: 1-891369-11-3. What it feels like the first time. "Inspiring reading." —*The Wall Street Journal.*

WOMEN RUNNERS: Stories of Transformation. Edited by Irene Reti and Bettianne Shoney Sien. Stories of how running has changed women's lives. 256 pages, hardcover, $23. ISBN: 1-891369-25-3

THE OTHER KINGDOM, by Victor Price. Classic Irish running novel about a young miler. 220 pages, paperback, $14.95. ISBN: 1-55821-451-8 "An intriguing novel concerning the metaphysics of sport, and of excellence in general." —*The New York Times Book Review*

THE QUOTABLE CYCLIST: Great Moments of Bicycling Wisdom, Inspiration, and Humor. 360 pages. $22 hardcover, ISBN 1-55821-563-8. $13 paperback, ISBN: 1-891369-27-X.

THE PENGUIN BRIGADE TRAINING LOG. *Runner's World* columnist John Bingham, hero to slow runners (penguins) everywhere, gives advice and exhortation in this useful training log. Spiral-bound, $14.95, 160 pages. ISBN: 1-55821-672-3.

BONE GAMES: Extreme Sports, Shamanism, Zen, and the Search for Transcendence, by Rob Schultheis. 188 pages, paperback, $12.95. ISBN: 1-55821-506-9. A fascinating inquiry into visionary, spiritual, and preternatural experiences induced by ultra-endurance sports.

THE WALKER'S LITERARY COMPANION, by Gilbert, Robinson, and Wallace. Great walks and walking in literature. $24, hardcover, 1-891369-19-9.

THE QUOTABLE WALKER: Great Moments of Wisdom and Inspiration for Walkers and Hikers. Edited by Roger Gilbert, Jeffrey Robinson, and Anne Wallace. All the wisest, funniest things said about bipedal locomotion. Hardcover, 288 pages, $22. ISBN: 1-891369-22-9

**In bookstores everywhere, or from Breakaway Books (800) 548-4348
See all our books at: www.breakawaybooks.com**